Killer Angel

Killer Angel

A Short Biography of
Planned Parenthood's Founder
Margaret Sanger

Revised Edition

George Grant

Cumberland House
Nashville, Tennessee

Published by Cumberland House Publishing, Inc.,
431 Harding Industrial Drive, Nashville, TN 37211

Cover design by Julia Pitkin
Text design by Mike Towle

Library of Congress Cataloging-in-Publication Data is available.

ISBN: 9781581821505

Printed in the United States of America
1 2 3 4 5 6 7 8 9—06 05 04 03 02 01

To Susan Hunt,
Angel of Hope,
and
To
Karen Grant

Contents

Foreword

THERE ARE MANY WHO would prefer that you not read this book, for in it George Grant masterfully exposes the pathology and psychology of the patron saint of America's abortion cult. The republication of this volume is not only timely, it is also desperately needed to provide an understanding of the widespread culture of death that permeates our society.

In *Killer Angel*, Grant deftly lays his intellectual scalpel to the soft underbelly of radical feminism in the persona of Margaret Sanger, Planned Parenthood's founder, and he lays open the philosophical underpinnings of a worldview that has led to the death of untold millions in the last century.

The events leading up to this edition of *Killer Angel* are nothing short of providential. It all began when a Toledo, Ohio, couple, Dean and Melanie Witt, donated two copies of a previous edition of *Killer Angel* to the Toledo-Lucas Public Library. The library initially accepted the book, only for it to be later banned after the library's central office staff intervened and rejected the book. A letter from the library to the Witts stated, "The author's political and social agenda, which is strongly espoused throughout the book, is not appropriate."

Not content with the library's seemingly arbitrary censorship standard determining what was or was not "appropriate," the Witts repeatedly requested clarification of the library's position. The officials within the library hierarchy met those requests with stony silence. After failing to receive an explanation for the library's ban of the book, and frustrated by the lack of response from library officials, the Witts forwarded documentation of the incident to Dr. Grant, who in turn passed the material on to me.

Upon receiving the documentation, I wrote an article about the library's censorship policies for WorldNetDaily.com, an independent investigative Internet news site. It has a daily readership in the hundreds of thousands and is a frequent resource for radio talk show hosts around the country.

While researching my article on *Killer Angel*'s ban, I discovered that the Toledo library's censorship decision violated the library's own material-selection statement, which says that "the Library collection shall include representative materials of all races and nationalities, and all political, religious, economic, and social views." Even when confronted by their own written policy prohibiting the very censorship they engaged in, officials from the library refused to comment for the story on their actions.

I also interviewed officials from the American Library Association (ALA), one of the cosponsors of the annual "Banned Books Week," for the article.

Judith Krug, the director of the ALA's Office of Intellectual Freedom (an example of pure Orwellian doublespeak), threw her support behind the library's decision to censor *Killer Angel*. She stated that librarians should be free to censor donated books and should have wide discretion in deciding what materials are included in the library's collection. Krug also said that the ALA's stand against book banning applied only after books had first passed librarian muster.

Upon publication of the story, news of the Toledo library's decision to censor *Killer Angel* spread rapidly, fueled by WorldNetDaily.com's large readership and subsequent discussion of the article by numerous talk radio hosts. Then talk radio giant Dr. Laura Schlessinger read the article in its entirety on her *Ask Dr. Laura* program, which drew nationwide attention to the controversy.

Blindsided by the exposé and faced with the mounting fallout from the WorldNetDaily.com article, the Toledo library's management ordered a media blackout by refusing to comment even to local TV news stations.

However, the library establishment across the nation immediately rallied its troops and rose to the Toledo library's defense. Internet bulletin boards and e-mail discussion groups frequented by library personnel buzzed with justification and defenses of library-imposed censorship. The decision to censor *Killer Angel* was also defended in the editorial pages of the local newspaper, the *Toledo Blade*.

The circumstances surrounding the republication of *Killer Angel* are a reflection of the larger religious and cultural battles manifest in our society today. Many people in our country would rather throttle the free

expression of their opponents than have their worldview
exposed for what it is.

With this in mind, the attempt to censor *Killer
Angel* is quite understandable. This is because Grant
clearly demonstrates that Sanger's virulent racism and
perverse lifestyle are not merely aberrations of an otherwise impeccable character, but are rather the direct
consequences of a humanistic faith rooted in radical
unbelief. The importance of this book and its discussion of Sanger ought to be seen in light of how this
radical unbelief pervades our culture as well as our
religious and civic institutions to the point that it is
now the predominant religion in America.

Most devotees of this humanist religion are intent
on concealing the logical outworking of this faith—
elitism, inegalitarianism, and tyranny, which contradict
the tolerant, pluralistic, and egalitarian public image
assumed by Sanger's followers. With Sanger as their
role model, public officials and private individuals are
now engaged in an active campaign to liberate man
from God's Law-Word and to subvert the remaining
freedoms that we in America continue to enjoy, all in
pursuit of that promise of old, "You shall be as God."
(Genesis 3:5).

For these reasons, Grant's thoroughly researched
and meticulous study of Margaret Sanger and her
legacy is needed now more than ever. Therefore, I
commend this edition of *Killer Angel* to the sober
judgment of the reader.

—*Patrick S. Poole*
Director of Alumni,
Blackstone Fellowship

Acknowledgments

"I am riding my pen on the shuffle, and it has a mouth of iron."

G. K. Chesterton[1]

Hᴵʟᴀɪʀᴇ Bᴇʟʟᴏᴄ, ᴘᴇʀʜᴀᴘs ᴛʜᴇ most prolific curmudgeon of this century, once quipped, "There is something odd book writers do in their prefaces, which is to introduce a mass of nincompoops of whom no one has ever heard, and say, *my thanks is due to such and such*, all in a litany, as though anyone cared a farthing for the rats."[2]

Belloc obviously did not place a lot of stock in either gratitude or accountability. His fierce self-assurance and autonomy as an author were defiantly unflappable. I would hope that I know better.

A number of friends and fellow-laborers encouraged me to pursue this project, and at the same time they helped support the work of the King's Meadow Study Center so that I could complete this. The

families of the Micah Class at Christ Community
Church, the yokefellows of the Empty Hands Fellowship, and the members of the Covenant Men's
Meeting guided me through many rocky shoals with
their wise counsel and friendship.

Mike Hyatt first suggested that I consider turning
my writing proclivities toward biographies. Jan
Dennis, David Dunham, Jim Bell, and Dean Andreola
gave me my first opportunities to try my hand at this
rather demanding art. Randy Terry suggested this particular project. And Otto Scott pointed the way for
me by providing the appropriate models from which
to learn.

Michael Schwartz, Jim Sedlak, Patricia Bainbridge,
and Doug Scott are among the finest thinkers, writers,
and researchers in the area of Planned Parenthood,
Margaret Sanger, and the abortion issue. Each has been
amazingly gracious and kind to me in sharing their
insights, resources, and information.

This revised edition was encouraged by Joseph
Farah, Pat Poole, and all of the other fine folks at
WorldNetDaily.com. One of the best arguments for the
proliferation of Internet access, WorldNetDaily.com is
arguably the most reliable media source of news and
information in recent memory—which is why, like tens
of thousands of others, I turn to it on a daily basis.

The soundtrack for this project was provided by
Loreena McKennitt, Clannad, Mychael Danna, and Jeff
Johnson, while the midnight musings were provided
by John Buchan, Colin Thubron, Samuel Johnson, and,
of course, G. K. Chesterton.

To all these, I offer my sincerest thanks.

I probably ought to mention as well the Nine

Muses, the Three Graces, and the Merry Band of Joyeuse Garde, but the fact is my greatest and best inspiration comes from my family. Karen is without a doubt a "helpmate" for me. And Joel, Joanna, and Jesse are the pride of my life. Their love and unwavering faithfulness remain my greatest hope and richest resource. To them I owe my all.

—*George Grant*
KingsMeadow.com

Introduction

"For all the apparent materialism and mass mechanism of our present culture, we, far more than any of our fathers, live in a world of shadows."

G. K. Chesterton[1]

On January 1, 1900, most Americans greeted the twentieth century with the proud and certain belief that the next hundred years would be the greatest, the most glorious, and the most glamorous in human history. They were infected with a sanguine spirit. Optimism was rampant. A brazen confidence colored their every activity.

Certainly, nothing in their experience could make them think otherwise. Never had a century changed the lives of men and women more dramatically than the previous one. The twentieth century moved fast and furiously, so much so that those of us who lived in it felt giddy sometimes, watching it spin; but the nineteenth century had actually moved faster and more furiously. Railroads, telephones, the telegraph, electricity,

mass production, forged steel, automobiles, and count-
less other modern discoveries had all come upon them
at a dizzying pace, expanding their visions and expecta-
tions far beyond their grandfathers' wildest dreams.

It was more than unfounded imagination, then,
that justified the New York World's New Year's predic-
tion that the twentieth century would "meet and overcome all perils and prove to be the best that this
steadily improving planet has ever seen."[2]

Most Americans were cheerfully assured that control of man and nature would soon be within their
grasp, and it would bestow upon them the unfathom-
able millennial power to alter the destinies of societies,
nations, and epochs. They were a people of manifold
purpose as well as manifest destiny.

They could not have known that dark and malignant seeds were germinating just beneath the surface
of the new century's soil. Josef Stalin at the time was a
twenty-one-year-old seminary student in Tiflis, a pious
and serene community located at the crossroads of
Georgia and Ukraine. Benito Mussolini was a seven-
teen-year-old student teacher in the quiet suburbs of
Milan. Adolf Hitler was an eleven-year-old aspiring art
student in the quaint upper Austrian village of Bran-
nan. And Margaret Sanger was a twenty-year-old, out-
of-sorts, nursing school dropout in White Plains, New
York. Who could have ever guessed on that ebulliently
auspicious New Year's Day that those four youngsters
would, over the span of the next century, spill more
innocent blood than all the murderers, warlords, and
tyrants of past history combined? Who could have
guessed that those four relative youths would together
ensure that the hopes, dreams, and aspirations of the

twentieth century would be smothered under holocaust, genocide, and triage?

As the champion of the proletariat, Stalin would see to the slaughter of at least fifteen million Russian and Ukrainian *kulaks*. As the popularly acclaimed *Il Duce*, Mussolini would massacre as many as four million Ethiopians, two million Eritreans, and a million Serbs, Croats, and Albanians. As the wildly lionized *Führer*, Hitler would exterminate more than six million Jews, two million Slavs, and a million Poles. As the founder of Planned Parenthood and the impassioned heroine of various feminist *causes célèbres*, Sanger would be responsible for the brutal elimination of more than thirty million children in the United States and as many as two and a half billion worldwide.

No one in his right mind would want to rehabilitate the reputations of Stalin, Mussolini, or Hitler. Their barbarism, treachery, and debauchery will make their names forever live in infamy. Amazingly, though, Sanger has somehow escaped this wretched fate. In spite of the fact that her crimes against humanity were no less heinous than theirs, her place in history has effectively been sanitized and sanctified. In spite of the fact that she openly identified herself in one way or another with the intentions, ideologies, and movements of the other three—Stalin's *Sobornostic Collectivism*, Hitler's *Eugenic Racism*, and Mussolini's *Agathistic Fascism*—Sanger's faithful minions have managed to manufacture an independent reputation for the perpetuation of her memory.

In life and death, the progenitor of the grisly abortion industry and the patron of the devastating sexual revolution has been lauded as a "radiant" and "courageous" reformer.[3] She has been heralded by friend and foe alike as "a heroine," "a champion," "a saint," and "a martyr."[4] Honored by men as different and divergent as H. G. Wells and Martin Luther King, George Bernard Shaw and Harry Truman, Bertrand Russell and John D. Rockefeller, Albert Einstein and Dwight Eisenhower, this remarkable "killer angel" was able to hide her perverse atrocities, while emerging in the annals of history practically vindicated and victorious.[5]

That this could happen is a scandal of grotesque proportions.

And recently the proportions have only grown— like a deleterious Kudzu or a rogue Topsy. Sanger has been the subject of adoring television dramas, hagiographical biographies, patronizing theatrical productions, and saccharined musical tributes. Though the facts of her life and work are anything but inspiring, millions of unwary moderns have been urged to find in them inspiration and hope. After all, myth is rarely based on truth.

Sanger's rehabilitation has been made possible by writers, journalists, historians, social scientists, and sundry other media celebrities steadfastly and selectively obscuring or blithely ignoring what she did, what she said, and what she believed. It has thus depended upon an ideological, don't-confuse-me-with-the-facts tenacity unmatched by any but the most extreme of our modern secular cults.

This brief monograph is an attempt to set the record straight. It is an attempt to rectify that shameful distortion of the social, cultural, and historical record. It has no other agenda than to replace fiction with fact.

Nevertheless, that agenda necessarily involves stripping away many layers of dense palimpsests of politically correct revisionism. But that ought to be the honest historian's central purpose anyway. Henry Cabot Lodge once asserted:

> Nearly all the historical work worth doing at the present moment in the English language is the work of shoveling off heaps of rubbish inherited from the immediate past.[6]

That, then, is the task of this book.

Many question the relevance of any kind of biographical or historical work at all. I can't even begin to recount how many times a Planned Parenthood staffer has tried to deflect the impact of Sanger's heinous record by dismissing it as "old news" or "ancient history" and thus irrelevant to any current issue or discussion.

It is an argument that seems to sell well in the current marketplace of ideas. We have actually come to believe that matters and persons of present import are unaffected by matters and persons of past import.

We moderns hold to a strangely disjunctive view of the relationship between life and work—thus enabling us to nonchalantly separate a person's private character from his or her public accomplishments. But this novel divorce of root from fruit, however genteel, is a ribald denial of one of the most basic truths in life: what you are begets what you do; wrongheaded philosophies stem from wrongheaded philosophers; sin doesn't just happen—it is sinners who sin.

Thus, according to the English historian and journalist Hilaire Belloc, "Biography always affords the greatest insights into sociology. To comprehend the history of a thing is to unlock the mysteries of its present, and more, to discover the profundities of its future."[7] Similarly, the inimitable Samuel Johnson quipped, "Almost all the miseries of life, almost all the wickedness that infects society, and almost all the distresses that afflict mankind, are the consequences of some defect in private duties."[8] Or, as E. Michael Jones has asserted, "Biography is destiny."[9]

This is particularly true in Margaret Sanger's case. The organization she founded, Planned Parenthood, is the oldest, largest, and best-organized provider of abortion and birth control services in the world.[10] From its ignoble beginnings near the turn of the century, when the entire shoestring operation consisted of an illegal back-alley clinic in a shabby Brooklyn neighborhood staffed by a shadowy clutch of firebrand activists and anarchists,[11] it has expanded dramatically. It is now a multibillion-dollar international conglomerate with programs and activities in 134 nations representing every continent. In the United States alone, it has mobilized more than 20,000 staff personnel and volunteers along the front lines of an increasingly confrontational and vitriolic culture war. Today they man the organization's 167 affiliates and its 922 clinics in virtually every major metropolitan area, coast to coast.[12] Boasting an opulent national headquarters in New York, a sedulous legislative center in Washington, opprobrious regional command posts in Atlanta, Chicago, Miami, and San Francisco, and officious international centers in London, Nairobi, Bangkok, and New Dehli, the federation showed $23.5 million in earnings during fiscal year 1992, with $192.9 million in cash reserves and another $108.2 million in capital assets.[13] With an estimated combined annual budget—including all regional and international service affiliates—of more than a trillion dollars, Planned Parenthood might well be the largest and most profitable nonprofit organization in history.[14]

The organization has used its considerable political, institutional, and financial clout to mainstream old-school, left-wing extremism. It has weighed in with sophisticated lobbying, advertising, and back room strong-arming to virtually remove the millennium-long stigma against child-killing abortion procedures and family-sundering socialization programs. Planned Parenthood thus looms like a Goliath over the increasingly tragic culture war.

Despite Planned Parenthood's leviathan proportions, it is impossible to entirely understand its policies, programs, and priorities apart from Margaret Sanger's life and work. It was, after all, originally established to be little more than an extension of her life and worldview.[15]

Most of the material from this project has been culled from research that I originally conducted for a comprehensive exposé of that vast institutional cash cow. Entitled *Grand Illusions: The Legacy of Planned Parenthood*, that book has gone through fourteen printings and four editions since it was first published in 1988.[16] It gave wide exposure to the tragic proportions of Sanger's saga. From the beginning of that project, though, I felt that a shorter and more carefully focused biographical treatment was warranted. Little has changed in the interim—except that the monolithic reputations of Sanger and her frighteningly dystopic organization have only been further enhanced.

It is therefore long overdue that the truth be told. It is long overdue that the proper standing of Margaret Sanger in the sordid history of this bloody century be secured. To that end, this book is written.

You can't help but notice, however, that it is a deliberately abbreviated tome—that is especially obvious when it is compared to the breadth and depth of its wellspring, *Grand Illusions*. Unpleasantries need to be accurately portrayed, but they need not be belabored. Caveats ought to be precise and to the point. Corrective counterblasts ought to be painstakingly careful, never crossing the all-too-fine line between informing and defiling the minds of readers.

You also can't help but notice that it is a deliberate throwback to the old form of historical writing: not so much a branch of dispassionate and objective science as a kind of purposeful moral philosophy. This premodern form is very apropos for this consummately postmodern subject.

Just as brevity and purpose are the heart and soul of wit, so they are the crux and culmination of true understanding. In light of this, it is my sincere prayer that true understanding will indeed be the end result of this brief but passionate effort.

Deus Vult.

PART I

STILL LIFE

"We perpetually come back to that sharp and shining point which the modern world is perpetually trying to avoid. We must have a creed, even in order to be comprehensive."

G. K. Chesterton[1]

I

Root of
Bitterness

"Happy is he who not only knows the causes of things but who has not lost touch with their beginnings."

G. K. Chesterton[2]

MARGARET SANGER WAS BORN the sixth of eleven children on September 14, 1879, in the small industrial community of Corning, in upstate New York. The circumstances of her home life were never happy—a fact to which she later attributed much of her agitated activism and bitter bombast. If it is true that "The hand that rocks the cradle rules the world," it is equally true that "The hand that wrecks the cradle ruins the world."[3]

Her father, Michael Higgins, was an Irish Catholic immigrant who fancied himself a radical freethinker and a freewheeling skeptic. As a youngster he had enlisted in General William Sherman's notorious Twelfth New York Cavalry, and proudly participated in the nefarious campaign that ravaged and ravished the South, across Tennessee, through Atlanta, and to the sea. He achieved notable infamy among his peers when he was honored by his commander for special treachery in fiercely subduing the recalcitrant captive population. Not surprisingly, that cruel and inhuman experience apparently hardened and embittered him. Triage and genocide are not easily forgotten by victims or perpetrators. His criminal inhumanity constituted a kind of spiritual calamity from which he, like so many others of his region, never fully recovered. Forever afterward he was pathetically stunted, unable to maintain even a modicum of normalcy in his life or relations.

Michael worked sporadically as a stonemason and a tombstone carver, but he was either unwilling or unable to adequately provide for his large family. Margaret's mother, Anne Purcell, was a second-generation American from a strict Irish Catholic family. She was frail and tuberculous but utterly devoted to her unstable, unpredictable husband—as well as their ever-growing brood of children.

The family suffered bitterly from cold, privation, and hunger. That was the common lot of thousands of other families in nineteenth-century America. But the Higginses also suffered grievously from scorn, shame, and isolation because of Michael's sullen improvidence. Like many men proudly progressive in public, he was repressively remonstrant at home. He regularly thrashed his sons "to make men of them."[4] He treated his wife and daughters as "virtual slaves."[5] And when he drank—which was whenever he could afford it—his volatile presence was even more oppressive than it normally was.

That is the paradox of dogmatic liberalism: though it loudly declares itself a champion of the weak, it is actually an unrelenting truncheon of the strong. Ideology inevitably resolves itself in some form of tyranny.

Margaret later described her family's existence under the unenlightened and inhuman hand of Michael's enlightened humanism as "joyless and filled with drudgery and fear."[6] Even as an adult, whenever she was on a train that merely rode through Corning, she got a sharp pain in the pit of her stomach. She suffered, she said, from "Corningitis."[7]

Clearly, the Higginses had an impoverished and isolated life. Not only did they have to endure grave social and material lack, they were spiritually deprived as well. As a confirmed skeptic, Michael mocked the sincere religious devotion of most of his neighbors. He openly embraced radicalism, socialism, and atheism. And he had little tolerance for the modicum of morality that his poor wife tried to instill in the lives of their hapless children.

One day, for example, when Margaret was on her knees praying the Lord's Prayer, she came to the phrase "Give us this day our daily bread," and her father snidely cut her off.

"Who were you talking to?" he demanded.

"To God," she replied innocently.

"Well, tell me, is God a baker?"

With no little consternation, she said, "No, of course not. But He makes the rain, the sunshine, and all the things that make the wheat, which makes the bread."

After a thoughtful pause her father rejoined, "Well, well, so that's the idea. Then why didn't you just say so? Always say what you mean, my daughter, it is much better."[8]

In spite of Michael's concerted efforts to undermine Margaret's young and fragile faith, her mother had her baptized in Saint Mary's Catholic Church on March 23, 1893. A year later, on July 8, 1894, she was confirmed. Both ceremonies were held in secret—her father would have been furious had he known. For some time afterward Margaret displayed a zealous devotion to spiritual things. She regularly attended services and observed the disciplines of the liturgical year. She demonstrated a budding and apparently authentic hunger for truth.

Gradually, the smothering effects of Michael's cynicism took their toll on young Margaret. When her mother died under the strain of her unhappy privation, Margaret was more vulnerable than ever before to her father's fierce undermining. Bitter, lonely, and grief-stricken, by the time she was seventeen her passion for Christ had collapsed into a bitter hatred of the Church. It was a malignant malevolence that would forever be her spiritual hallmark.

Anxious to move away from her malignant home life as soon as she could, Margaret was practically willing to go anywhere and try anything—as long as it was far from Corning. After a quick, almost frantic search, she settled on Claverack College. A small and inexpensive coeducational boarding school attached to the famed Hudson River Institute, Claverack was a Methodist high school housed in an imposing wooden building on twenty picturesque acres overlooking the

Hudson Valley. Not known for its academic rigors, the school was essentially a finishing school for protean youth.

It was at Claverack that Margaret got her first taste of freedom. And what a wild and intoxicating freedom it was. She plunged into radical politics, suffragette feminism, and unfettered sex. Despite her relatively light academic load, she quickly fell behind in her work. She rarely attended her classes. And she almost never completed her assignments. Worse, she neglected her part-time job—necessary to pay for the nominal tuition.

It is said that we become most like those against whom we are bitter. Despite her now obvious animosity toward her father, Margaret began to unconsciously emulate his erratic personality. The more her resistance to his influence grew, the greater her imitation of his improvidence became.

But character has consequences. When she could no longer afford the tuition at Claverack, Margaret was forced to return home—but only long enough to gather her belongings and set her affairs in order. She had drunk from the cup of concupiscence and would never again be satisfied with the quiet responsibilities and virtues of domesticity. As soon as she could, she moved in with her older sister in White Plains, taking a job there as a kindergarten teacher. A youth corrupted had become a youth corrupter.

Since she herself was now a high school dropout, she was assigned to a class consisting primarily of children of new immigrants. Much to her dismay, she found that her pupils couldn't understand a word that she said. She quickly grew tired of the laborious routine of teaching day in and day out. Gratefully, she quit after just two short terms.

Next, she applied for a job as a nurse-probationer at a small local hospital. Again, though, Margaret's careless and nomadic rootlessness was telling. Hospital work proved to be even more vexing and taxing than teaching. She never finished her training.

In later years she would claim to be a trained and practiced nurse. Nearly forty pages of her autobiography were devoted to her varied, often heroic, experiences as a seasoned veteran in professional health care.[9] But they were little more than Margaret's well-realized fantasies.

In fact, her actual exposure to medicine was almost nonexistent: she never got beyond running errands, changing sheets, and emptying bedpans. Like so much else in the mythic fable of her rise to prominence, her career as a nurse was little more than perpetrated fraud.

Determined to escape from the harsh bondage of labor and industry, she once again began to cast about for some viable alternative. She finally resorted to the only viable course open to a poor girl in those seemingly unenlightened days when the Puritan Work Ethic was still ethical: she married into money.

2

The Winter of Her Discontent

"The special mark of the modern world is not that it is skeptical, but that it is dogmatic without knowing it."

G. K. Chesterton[1]

WILLIAM SANGER WASN'T EXACTLY rich, but he was financially secure—and for Margaret that was close enough. He was a young man of great promise. An up-and-coming architect with the famed New York City firm of McKim, Mead, and White, he had already made a name for himself while working on the plans for the resplendent Grand Central Station and the landmark Woolworth tower in Midtown Manhattan.

He met Margaret at a party in White Plains in 1900 and immediately fell head over heels in love. He was a tall, dark-haired man with intense coal-black eyes and a thin-set mouth turned down like an eagle's. Now almost thirty and entirely dedicated to his work, he had sorely neglected the social side of his life for several years. But he was smitten by the girlishly slim, redheaded beauty he met that day.

William courted Margaret with a single-minded zeal, promising her devotion, leisure, and a beautiful home—the fulfillment of her most cherished dreams. He plied her affections with flowers, candy, jewelry, and unremitting attention. As for her part, she was willingly—even enthusiastically—courted.

Within just a few months, they were married.

The Sangers settled into a pleasant apartment in Manhattan's Upper East Side and set up housekeeping. But housekeeping appealed to Margaret even less than teaching or nursing. Though she busied herself collecting pots, pans, and dishes, she quickly grew restless and sullen.

Her doting husband tried everything he could think of in a determined effort to find a way to satisfy her restless and unresolved passions. He sent her off for long vacations in the Adirondacks. He hired maids and attendants. He bought her expensive presents. He even designed and built an extravagant home in the exclusive Long Island suburbs. Nothing, however, could suit his temperamental bride.

In short order they had three children, two boys and a girl. Like so many mothers before and since, Margaret thought that having babies might bring her the fulfillment she so longed for. Raising children is not exactly a hobby to be taken on a whim by the discontented. It is a responsible commitment requiring diligence, long-suffering, and hard work. Margaret had never been one to apply herself to such disciplines. Alas, even her children proved to be but temporary diversions.

Once again, she demonstrated the telling truth of tired truism: like father, like daughter.

After nearly a decade of undefined domestic discontent, she convinced William to sell all they had, including their comfortable suburban estate, and move back into the brusque and cosmopolitan Manhattan hubbub.

She quickly threw herself into the fast-paced social life of the city: shopping, dining, reveling, and theater-going. She attempted to drown her rootless discontent in the wastrel champagne of improvidence.

Meanwhile, William began to renew old ties in radical politics by attending Socialist, Anarchist, and Communist meetings in Greenwich Village. Before he wooed Margaret, he had toyed with adolescent notions of political millenarianism and social utopianism from time to time. With his wife distracted by her material quest and his work no longer an all-consuming passion, he once again explored the nether realm of coercive idealism.

At the time New York was well on its way to becoming a seething cauldron of radical ideas and social unrest. The syndicalist notions of the early labor movement, the libertarian ideas of the early suffragette movement, and the proletarian notions of the early progressive movement made for a heady cultural brew. And William drank from it deeply. He threw in his lot with myriad extremist groups, fringe coalitions, and perennial lost causes.

Though Margaret generally eschewed the smoke-filled rooms and the fervid rhetoric of Williams's radical associations, from time to time—usually when she bored of her more patrician activities—Margaret would tag along with William to sundry rallies, caucuses, and protests. Though his sense of justice and social ire seemed perpetually roused to a fever pitch, she remained supremely unimpressed. In fact, she often mocked the ragtag revolutionaries as the comical and motley crew that they were. She described Bill Haywood, founder of the left-wing Industrial Workers of the World, as "an uncouth, stumbling, one-eyed giant with an enormous head."[2] She said that Alexander Beckman, another perennially hapless labor organizer from the radical fringe, was essentially "a hack, armchair socialist—full of hot air but likely little else."[3] She called Eugene Debs a "silly silk hat radical."[4] And she characterized the partisans of the Socialist Party as "losers, complainers, and perpetual victims—unwilling or unable to do for themselves, much less for society at large."[5]

One evening, however, she heard a radical labor organizer describe the pitiful working conditions of the many sweatshops and chattel-dens throughout New York's Lower West Side and the Midtown Garment District. But it wasn't really the image of suffering and injustice that arrested her attentions—she had heard all that before. It was the speaker's vision of the power of well-planned social subversion and disruptive antiestablishment protest that gripped her.

John Reed, who would later gain fame as a propagandist for the Bolsheviks in Soviet Russia, was a passionate speaker who exuded confidence. He also had a knack for vivid, compelling prose. He described with heroic idealism a kind of ideological crusade bent on irreverently overturning the privileged status quo. Appealing to Margaret's romantic extremism, he painted a lucidly resplendent picture of adventurous anarchy akin to some prediluvian epoch.

Margaret was awestruck. The ideas and ideals of Marxism had never seemed particularly relevant to the real world. But in the hands of a compelling presence like Reed, they came alive to her. Before long, she could think of little else. She was completely radicalized.

She suddenly shed her bourgeois habits in favor of Bohemian ways. Instead of whiling away the hours in the elegant shops along Fifth Avenue, she plunged headlong into the maelstrom of rebellion and revolution.

She read voraciously—for the first time in her life. John Spargo had just translated Marx's *Das Capital* into English. Lincoln Steffens had published *The Shame of the Cities*. Jacob Riis released his classic, *How the Other Half Lives*. Upton Sinclair was shaking the establishment with raging indictments like *The Jungle*. And George Fitzpatrick produced *War, What For?* Each became an important factor in the development of her newfound interests.

And each became an important part of William and Margaret's lifestyle, too—their apartment quickly became a social hub for the various legions of the hodgepodge revolutionaries. Those whom she once scorned as "fanatics" and "misfits" became a regaled coterie in their home.

She later wrote:

> Our living room became a gathering place where liberals, anarchists, Socialists, and IWW's could meet. These vehement individualists had

to have an audience, preferably a small, inti-
mate one. Any evening you might find visitors
being aroused by Jack Reed, bullied by Bill Haywood, or led softly towards anarchism by Alex
Berkman. When throats grew dry and the flood
of oratory waned, someone went out for ham-
burgers, sandwiches, hot dogs, and beer. The
luxuriousness of the midnight repast depended
upon the collection of coins tossed into the
middle of the table, which consisted of what
everybody had in his pocket. Those were halcyon days, indeed.[6]

During those halcyon days, Margaret underwent a
transformation no less dramatic than might be
expected of a religious convert. She was a zealot. Even
the breathy cabaret of her brazenness became subject
to the revolutionary cause. In her, softer needs seemed
now to be stillborn. She became as resolute and unrelenting as permafrost.

Like a medieval mystic or cabalistic alchemist, her
every waking moment was dominated by thoughts of
ushering the great utopia—by whatever wrenching
means were necessary. Violence. Sabotage. Assassination. Subversion. Insurrection. Terror. These became
the stock-in-trade of her born-again, left-wing funda-
mentalism.

And this was no passing fancy—her conversion
proved to be genuine. For the rest of her long life every
other concern was subordinated to *the cause*.

Part II

WHENCE?
WHAT?
WHITHER?

"There is a tradition that jumping off a precipice is prejudicial to the health; and therefore nobody does it. Then appears a progressive prophet and reformer, who points out that we really know nothing about it, because nobody does it. And the tradition is thereby mocked—to the peril of us all."

G. K. Chesterton[1]

3

THE WOMAN REBEL

"What seems to infect the modern world is a sort of swollen pride in the possession of modern thought or free thought or higher thought, combined with a comparative neglect of thought."

G. K. Chesterton[2]

A T FIRST, WILLIAM WAS thrilled by Margaret's sudden conversion. It seemed that his bride had at last found her long-sought-after meaning, purpose, and fulfillment.

She was now forever hatching subversive plots, railing against hidden conspiracies, inciting invectives against the authorities, and ingratiating herself to the foremost radicals of the day: John Reed, Eugene Debs, Clarence Darrow, Will Durant, Upton Sinclair, Julius Hammer, and Bill Haywood. Like a sycophant courtier, she was an omnipresent whirlwind of energy and starry-eyed adulation.

She joined the *de rigueur* Socialist Party and attended all of its functions. She even volunteered as a women's union organizer for the Party's infamous Local Number Five, speaking at labor organization meetings, and she began writing editorials and reviews for the Party newspaper, *The Call.*

By this time, virtually all of the most extreme revolutionary elements of American political life had been unified in the Socialist Party: the Radical Republicans, the Reformist Unitarians, the Knights of Labor, the Mugwumps, the Anarchists, the Populists, the Progressivists, the Suffragettes, the Single Taxers, the Grangers, and the Communists. Though it never moved much beyond the fringes of the nation's electoral experience, the Socialist Party was able to tap into the anomie and ennui of a significant segment of America's disenfranchised class. Its numbers swelled from ten thousand members in 1901 to fifty-eight thousand by 1908. More than twice that number was recorded four years later. And its voting strength was many times greater even than that, accounting for more than 6 percent of all the votes cast in the disastrously fractious national elections of 1912.

When Margaret and William Sanger entered the fray that year, the Party had elected twelve hundred public officials in thirty-three states and one hundred sixty cities, and it regularly published as many as three hundred tabloids, broadsides, and periodicals. It was progressive. It was visionary. And it was making headway among voters whose interests and fortunes had waned under the monopolistic grip of industrial mer-

cantilism. Socialism has always been a peculiar tempta-
tion for disenchanted American voters for whom brash
talk of equality is a tenet of faith and justice is a badge
of honor.

A significant source of the attraction during Margaret's halcyon revolutionary days was the personal
charisma of the "silly, silk hat radical," Eugene Debs. A
former railway worker and union organizer, Debs had
become the personification of socialism for most Americans. He had run at the top of the Party's ticket in five
different presidential campaigns—spanning a quarter-
century of the nation's greatest unrest and upheaval.
He became wildly popular among the disaffected as a
thoughtful and plainspoken champion of the ordinary
worker.

His rhetorical appeal was hardly unique—it was,
in fact, rooted in the standard material determinist fare
of the day. He claimed that the laborer and farmer were
oppressed victims of capitalism with its trusts, industrial tycoons, utilities magnates, large property owners,
a corrupt and controlled Congress, and the unem-
ployed. He decried the culturewide atmosphere of
intolerance, injustice, and heartless greed.

To remedy all these ills, Debs offered the scientific
and reasoned alternatives of a "managed economy," a
"widely distributed means of production," an "accessi-
ble health-care provision system," and an "ideal soviet-
ized central state."[3] He boldly declared that he was
"in revolt against capitalism."[4] In fact, he declared an
ideological war against all conventional politicians
within that system, saying:

> With every drop of blood in my veins, I despise
> their laws, and I will defy them. I am going

to speak to you as a Socialist, a Revolutionist,
and as a Bolshevist, if you please. The
Socialist Party stands fearlessly and uncompro-
misingly for the overthrow of the labor-rob-
bing, war-breeding, and crime-inciting
capitalist system.[5]

Later he would aid and abet the Russian Revolution, and he claimed that its success was "the greatest
single achievement in all history."[6] He said:

I am a Bolshevik. I am fighting for the same
thing here as they are fighting for over there. It
is essential that we affiliate with the Third
International, and without qualification.
Therein lies the hope of the future.[7]

From the vantage of the post-Cold War era, such
sentiments sound terribly naive and wrongheaded—
despite the fact that they remain the currency of what's
left of the Left—but during the tumultuous days just
after the War Between the States and before the First
World War, they were sentiments shared by a growing
segment of idealistic Americans.

Debs was the perennial underdog, willing to pay
any price for his convictions. His faithful followers
perceived him as the incorruptible voice of the people.
His oft-repeated pledge became populism's epigram-
matic byword: "While there is still a lower class, I am
in it; while there is a criminal element, I am of it;
while there is a soul in prison, I am not free."[8] Indeed,
he had to run one of his presidential bids from a cell
in the federal penitentiary after he was convicted of
sedition.

Debs not only gave socialism a human face, he gave it a heroic cast.

For that reason, Margaret became a passionate partisan. In addition, though, the record of Debs and the Party on women's issues impressed her. No other political movement in American history had fought so consistently for women's suffrage, sexual liberation, feminism, and birth control.

These subjects were a central aspect of the creedal dogma of the Party, and they had practically become obsessions for Margaret. And they made her commitment to ushering in a socialist revolution—regardless of the material or human cost necessary—all the more urgent.

While William was happy that Margaret had finally found a cause that satisfied her restless spirit, he gradually became concerned that she was perhaps taking on too much too soon. Her transformation was disconcertingly complete. Their apartment was in a perpetual state of disarray. Their children were constantly being farmed out to friends and neighbors. And their time alone together was nonexistent. While Margaret had never been particularly domestic and had never actually applied herself to making their house a home, her all-consuming political fanaticism had dispatched the family's needs altogether. William could not help but be concerned.

Jerry Talmadge was a friend of the Sangers—he worked with William at the architectural firm and volunteered his time with Margaret at various Socialist Party functions. He witnessed both the transformation of Margaret's passions and the escalation of William's concerns. Later he would write:

> It was rather sad. She was like a raging river
> overflowing the banks of conventionality and
> propriety. He was like the small householder
> attempting vainly to keep the floods from
> washing away his home and property. It was
> inevitable that the two would be at odds, one
> with another.[9]

It was bad enough that Margaret had become
entirely enamored with Debs and his comprehensive
dogma of revolution, but then when she fell under the
spell of the militant utopian Emma Goldman, William's husbandly concern turned to extreme disapproval. Almost overnight Margaret had gone from
archetypical material girl to revolutionary firebrand.
And now she was taking her cues from one of the most
dangerous and controversial insurrectionists since the
bloody Reign of Terror during the French Revolution.

It was just too much.

William began backpedaling furiously. He steered
clear of his radical associations. And he tried desperately to pull his wife back into a more conventional
social orbit. Now that the revolution had moved
beyond parlor fantasies and armchair bombast and
into the inner sanctum of his home and family, its
horrific disruptiveness became all too obvious to
him.

To Margaret's way of thinking, he had become a
traitor to *the cause*. She was now a true believer and
nothing and no one could possibly be allowed to interfere with its progress among men and nations. Thus,
the paranoia of fanaticism sorely stigmatized him in
her eyes.

And her new attachment to the steely determin-ism of Emma Goldman only reinforced that perversely held taint.

4

ΠΑΔΟΠΠΑ

*"Clichés are things that can be new and already old.
They are things that can be new and already dead. They
are the stillborn fruits of culture."*

G. K. Chesterton[1]

E MMA GOLDMAN WAS A fiery renegade who had close
connections with revolutionaries all over the
world: Bolsheviks in Russia, Fabians in England,
Anarchists in Germany, and Malthusians in France.
She drew large crowds while lecturing all across the
American heartland, discoursing on everything from
the necessity of free love to the nobility of incendiary
violence, from the evils of capitalism to the virtues of
assassination, from the perils of democracy to the
need for birth control.

She made her living selling her Anarchist magazine *Mother Earth* and by distributing leaflets on

contraception and liberated sex. Known as "the Red Queen of Anarchy," she was baleful and brutal. But she was brilliant—and she was more than capable of communicating that brilliance to vast throngs in her political rallies. Her spare, spartan appearance proved an apropos guise for her mechanistic dogma of dystopic disruption.

Margaret was completely taken by Goldman's erudite discussions of philosophical profundities and ideological certainties. She hung on Goldman's every word and began to read everything in Goldman's wide-ranging library of incendiary literature, including the massive, seven-volume *Studies in the Psychology of Sex* by Havelock Ellis, which stirred in her a new lust for lust.

Goldman discipled the young reformer, introducing her to the concupiscence of Ibsen, Tolstoy, Voltaire, and Kropotkin. She taught Margaret the grassroots mobilization tactics of the great revolutionary cabals of France, Austria, Poland, and Russia. She tutored her subversive impulse with the Enlightenment catechisms of Rousseau, Babeuf, Buonarroti, Nechayev, and Lenin. She reacquainted her with the subversive strategies of the Radical Republicans during the Reconstruction subjection of conquered territory following the American War Between the States. She schooled her in the verities of Humanism—the fantastic notions of the self-sufficiency and inherent goodness of man, the persistent hope of perfectibility, and the relativity of all ethical mores. She desensitized her to the most extreme ideas and the most perverse confabulations ever devised by men. She initiated her to their collusive mumblings as a druid would beadle an acolyte into the deepest darkness.

Not long into this ritualized initiation into the occult of ideological revolution, Margaret told her bewildered husband that she needed emancipation from every taint of Christianized capitalism—including the strict bonds of the marriage bed. She even suggested to him that they seriously consider experimenting with various trysts, infidelities, fornications, and adulteries. Because of her careful tutoring in socialist dogma, she had undergone a sexual liberation—at least intellectually—and she was now ready to test its authenticity physically.

He was shocked. And not surprisingly, he was deeply hurt.

In a desperate attempt to save their marriage, he rented a cottage on Cape Cod and took Margaret and the children for a long vacation. They rested and relaxed and played. They ate and drank and socialized.

By the time they returned, Goldman had departed the Bohemian scene in Greenwich Village for a speaking tour, and Margaret's attentions were deflected from the promiscuity of revolution, at least for the moment. She continued reading the radical and sensual literature of Ellis and others, but her activism gradually took a new and different turn.

A strike of textile workers in Lawrence, Massachusetts, drew the attention of Socialist sympathizers all over the country. Sponsored by a militantly Marxist union, the Industrial Workers of the World—or the IWW as it was more commonly known—the strike was seen by partisans as a tremendous chance to bring the revolution to the streets of America. Bill Haywood, the labor leader who had opportunistically formed the union after a series of sweatshop disasters, came to Greenwich Village looking for professional organizers to help him manage the strike.

Margaret jumped at the chance.

Her great tenacity, unswerving commitment, and innocent winsomeness proved to be tremendous assets for Haywood. She was able to stir up a great deal of sympathetic publicity. As a result the strike was a tremendous success. In fact, it may have been too successful. It had actually attracted the sympathies of several key industrialists, financiers, media outlets, entertainment moguls, and government officials. Even President Taft voiced his support for the workers and their cause. The battle was won, but the war was lost—the revolution never made it to the streets simply because the anger of the rebellion was diffused by the acceptance of the establishment. The IWW was unable to recover from its victory and was never again able to stage a successful strike.

Margaret returned to William and the children, despondent and discouraged.

In the weeks that followed, she was at a loss as to how to occupy her time. She busied herself by dabbling in amateur midwifery by day and by holding court in Mabel Dodge's salon by night.

Idle hands are the devil's playthings.

Dodge was a wealthy young divorcée, recently returned from France, where she had spent most of her married years. She had a stunning Fifth Avenue apartment in which she started a salon modeled after those in the Palais Royale and Paris's Left Bank. Her evening gatherings became regular opportunities for intellectuals, radicals, artists, actors, writers, and activists to

meet and greet, aspire and conspire. Each night had its
own theme: sometimes it would be politics, sometimes
drama, or perhaps poetry or economics or art or science. Ideas and liquor flowed freely until midnight,
when Dodge would usher in a sumptuous meal of the
finest meats, poultry, cheeses, and French pastries.

Margaret's topic of discussion was always sex. Her
detour into labor activism had done little to dampen
her interest in the subject. When it was her turn to
lead an evening, she held Dodge's guests spellbound,
ravaging their imaginations with intoxicating notions
of the aromatic dignity, the unfettered self-expression,
and the innate sacredness of sexual desire.

Avant-garde intellectuals in the Village had been
quietly practicing free love for years. Eugene O'Neill
took one mistress after another, immortalizing them
in his plays. Edna St. Vincent Millay hopped gaily
from bed to bed and wrote about it in her poems. Max
Eastman, Emma Goldman, Floyd Dell, Rockwell Kent,
Edgar Lee Masters, and many others had for some
time enjoyed unrestrained sexploits. But no one had
championed sexual freedom as openly and ardently as
Margaret. When she spoke, the others became trans-
fixed. Her innocent girl-next-door looks belied her
bordello motif and gutter talk. Dodge was especially
struck by her sensuous didactics. Later she would
write in her memoirs:

> Margaret Sanger was a Madonna type of
> woman, with soft reddish-brown hair parted
> over a quiet brow, and crystal-clear brown
> eyes. It was she who introduced us all to the
> idea of birth control, and it, along with other
> related ideas about sex, became her passion.

> It was as if she had been more or less arbi-
> trarily chosen by the powers-that-be to voice
> a new gospel of not only sex-knowledge in
> regard to conception, but also sex-knowledge
> in regard to copulation and its intrinsic
> importance. She was the first person I ever
> knew who was openly an ardent propagan-
> dist for the joys of the flesh. This, in those
> days, was radical indeed when the sense of
> sin was still so indubitably mixed with the
> sense of pleasure. Margaret personally set out
> to rehabilitate sex. She was one of its first
> conscious promulgators.[2]

In the safe environs of the Greenwich Village salon, surrounded by her radical peers, Margaret honed her promiscuous and lascivious shtick. She set the stage for a lifetime of sexual titillation and experimentation—a life sadly bereft of covenantal commitment.

For her, the success of the social revolution began with the sexual revolution. If *the cause* were ever to prevail culturally, it had to first prevail interpersonally through the unleashing of carnal passion. If the workers of the world were to unite, then the antiquated morals that suppressed their true innermost feelings and inhibited their true heartfelt expressions had to be eliminated.

It was not worth the terrible spiritual and emotional sacrifice, of course. But there was no telling Margaret. She was nothing short of hell-bent.

Part III

No Little People

> "We often hear of a man becoming a criminal through a love of low company. I believe it is much commoner for a man to become a criminal through a love of refined company. There is a kind of people who cannot stand poverty because they cannot stand ugliness. These people might rob or even murder out of pure refinement."
>
> G. K. Chesterton[1]

5

ARRESTED DEVELOPMENT

"Unless a man becomes the enemy of an evil, he will not even become its slave but rather its champion."

G. K. Chesterton[2]

EVERYONE WAS DELIGHTED BY Margaret's explicit and brazen talks. Everyone, that is, except her husband. William began to see the socialist revolution as nothing more than "an excuse for a saturnalia of sex."[3] He decided he had best get Margaret away once again.

This time he took Margaret and the children to Paris. He could pursue his newly developed interests in modern art. Margaret could study her now keen fascination with the advanced contraceptive methods widely available in France. And together they could

refresh their commitment to each other in the world's
most romantic city.

At first the ploy seemed to work. Together they
enjoyed the enchantments of the chattering solons,
the quaint artists' colonies, and quirky galleries that
dotted the Left Bank in those preholocaust, halcyon
days. They were awed by the magnificent fountains
that to this day fall with hallowed delicacy into the
framing space of the Place de la Concorde. They
gawked as blue hues crept out from behind the Col-
onnades in the Rue de Rivoli and through the grill-
work of the Tuileries. They marveled at the low
elegant outlines of the Louvre—a serious metallic
gray against the setting sun. They strolled under the
well-tended branches hung brooding over animated
cafes, embracing their conversations with tender inti-
macy. They reveled in the sight of the long windows
that opened onto ironclad balconies in marvelously
archaic hotels, while gauzy lace curtains fluttered
across imagined hopes and wishes and dreams.
Romance wafted freely in the sweet cool breezes off
the Seine—and the Sangers embraced it deeply and
passionately.

They took an apartment in a wonderful eighteenth-
century building replete with high ceilings, orna-
mented plaster bas-relief across one wall, huge
shuttered windows, antique furniture, and loads of
dusty old books. They surrounded themselves with all
the odd trappings of an ex-patriot's existence.

On their tight budget they couldn't afford the typ-
ical Grand Tour initiation to the city—sitting in the
chic cafes along the Champs Elysees for hours sip-
ping champagne at twelve dollars a glass, or buying

leather at Louis Vuitton at a thousand dollars per garment, or snatching up two-hundred-dollar scarves at Hermes, or eating at the Epicurean five-star Bristol Hotel at more than three hundred dollars a meal. Nonetheless, the pleasures of Paris could be had on an economy scale.

Each day they wandered over to the Pont Neuf bridge to explore the wares of the *bouquinistes*—the traditional French booksellers who in the early seventeenth century had pioneered their unique brand of transportable trade. William and Margaret would then visit one of the many magnificent museums or perhaps eat a picnic lunch in the Bois de Boulogne, the huge park along the city's western ridge. Often they would end up soaking in the jubilant carnival atmosphere at the Champs de Mars just below the Eiffel Tower.

Nowhere does the novelist's prose slip more readily into the bland tones of the travel guidebook. Paris is a marvel of vintage sensory delights, and both Margaret and William drank deeply from its draft. The staccato sounds of the clinking of saucers in the Place de la Contrescarpe, the trumpeting of traffic around the Arch de Triumph, and the conspiratorial whispering on benches in the Jardin de Luxembourg together played a jangling Debussy score in the twilight hours. The nostalgic smells of luxuriant perfumes, wine, and brandy; the invigorating odors of croissants, espresso, and cut lavender; and the acrid fumes of tobacco, roasted chestnuts, and salon sautés seemed to texture a sweet and subtle Monet upon the canvas of *l'entente de la vie*. The dominating sights of the yellow towers of Notre Dame, the arched bridges cutting across the satin sheen of the river, and the stately elegance of the Bourbon palaces and pavilions scattered about the city like caches of mercy seemed to sculpt a muscular Rodin bronze on the *tabla rasa* landscape.

It was almost heaven.

Almost. But not quite.

Victor Hugo, who loved the city with a passion, warned that the rich atmosphere of Parisian culture was deceptively intoxicating. He often asserted that "No one can spend any length of time in Paris without being captivated by satyrs or muses or cupids or baccuses or all of them together."[4]

Margaret *was* captivated by all of them together. The lure of revolutionary promiscuity beckoned her fiercely—and it seemed that the romance of Paris only intensified that siren's song. It was only a matter of time before she became anxious for her Village causes, friends, and lovers. She begged William to return to New York.

He refused. After a bitter flap—both of them adamant and unyielding—she simply abandoned him there, and returned to New York with the confused children in tow. He bid her good riddance—at last resigned to the fact that there was no longer any hope of salvaging the marriage.

Without her husband to support her every whim and fancy, Margaret was forced to find some means of providing an income for herself and the children. She had continued to write for *The Call* and found some degree of satisfaction in that, so she decided to try her hand at writing and publishing a paper herself.

She called it *The Woman Rebel*. It was an eight-sheet pulp with the slogan "No Gods and No Masters" emblazoned across the masthead. She advertised it as "a paper of militant thought."[5]

And militant it was indeed. The first issue denounced marriage as "a degenerate institution," capitalism as "indecent exploitation," and sexual modesty as "obscene prudery."[6] In the next issue, an article entitled "A Woman's Duty" proclaimed that "rebel women" were to "look the whole world in the face with a go-to-hell look in the eyes."[7] Another article asserted that "Rebel women claim the following rights: the right to be lazy, the right to be an unmarried mother, the right to destroy . . . and the right to love."[8] In later issues, she published several articles on contraception, several more on sexual liberation, three on the necessity for social revolution, and two defending political assassinations.[9]

The Woman Rebel was militant, all right. In fact, it was so militant that Margaret was promptly served with a subpoena indicting her on three counts for the publication of lewd and indecent articles in violation of the federal Comstock Laws.

The Comstock Laws had been passed by Congress in 1873. Their purpose was to close the mails to "obscene and lascivious" material, particularly erotic postcards and pornographic magazines from Europe which, during the debauched and confused postwar and Radical Reconstruction period, flooded the country. Anthony Comstock, their chief sponsor, was appointed a special agent of the Post Office, with the power to see that it was strictly enforced. For nearly half a century he fought an almost single-handed campaign to "keep the mails clean" and to "ensure just condemnation for the purveyors of filth, eroticism, and degeneracy."[10]

If convicted—and conviction was practically a foregone conclusion—Margaret could be sentenced to as much as five years in the federal penitentiary. Frightened, she obtained several extensions of her court date. But then, deciding that her case was hopeless, she determined to flee the country under an assumed name. She had her socialist friends forge a passport, secure passage across the border, provide her with connections and contacts in Canada and England, and take charge of her now inconvenient children.

As a final gesture, just before she secretly slipped out of the country, she had them print and distribute one hundred thousand copies of *Family Limitation*, a contraband leaflet on contraception that she had written. It was lurid and lascivious, designed to enrage the postal authorities and titillate the masses. But worse, it was dangerously inaccurate, recommending such things as "Lysol douches," "bichloride of mercury elixirs," "heavy doses of laxatives," and "herbal abortifacients."

Margaret Sanger's dubious career as the "champion of birth control" and "patron saint of feminism" was now well underway.

6

BABYLONIAN EXILE

"Under all its parade of novelty, the modern world really
runs to monotony, partly because it runs to monopoly."

G. K. Chesterton[1]

MARGARET SPENT MORE THAN a year in England as a fugitive from justice. But she made certain that the time was not wasted. She had found her key to *the cause*: revolutionary socialism. She had found her niche in *the cause*: sexual liberation. And now she would further *the cause* with a single-minded zeal.

As soon as she came ashore in England, Margaret started contacting the various radical groups of Britain. She began attending socialist lectures on Nietzsche's moral relativism, anarchist lectures on Kropotkin's sub-

versive pragmatism, and communist lectures on
Bakunin's collectivistic rationalism. But she was especially interested in developing close ties with the Malthusians.

Thomas Malthus was a nineteenth-century cleric
and part-time professor of political economy whose theories of population growth and economic stability
quickly became the basis for national and international
social policy throughout the West. Malthus theorized
that population grows exponentially over time, while
production grows only arithmetically. He believed a
crisis was inevitable—a kind of population time bomb
was ticking that he believed threatened the very existence of the human race. Poverty, deprivation, and
hunger were the evidences of this looming population
crisis. He believed that the only responsible social policy
would be one that addressed the unnatural problem of
population growth—by whatever means necessary.
Every social problem was subordinate to this central
cause. In fact, Malthus argued, to deal with sickness,
crime, privation, and need in any other way simply
aggravates the problems further—thus, he actually con-
demned charity, philanthropy, international relief and
development, missionary outreaches, and economic
investment around the world as counter-productive.

In his magnum opus, *An Essay on the Principle of
Population*, published in six editions between 1798 and
1826, Malthus wrote:

> All children born, beyond what would be
> required to keep up the population to a desired
> level, must necessarily perish, unless room be
> made for them by the deaths of grown persons
> . . . Therefore . . . we should facilitate, instead

of foolishly and vainly endeavoring to impede, the operations of nature in producing this mortality; and if we dread the too-frequent visitation of the horrid form of famine, we should sedulously encourage the other forms of destruction, which we compel nature to use. Instead of recommending cleanliness to the poor, we should encourage contrary habits. In our towns we should make the streets narrower, crowd more people into the houses, and court the return of the plague. In the country, we should build our villages near stagnant pools, and particularly encourage settlements in all marshy and unwholesome situations. But above all, we should reprobate specific remedies for ravaging diseases; and restrain those benevolent, but much mistaken men, who have thought they were doing a service to mankind by projecting schemes for the total extirpation of particular disorders.[2]

Malthus's disciples—the Malthusians and the Neo-Malthusians—believed that if Western civilization were to survive, the physically unfit, the materially poor, the spiritually diseased, the racially inferior, and the mentally incompetent had to somehow be suppressed and isolated—or perhaps even eliminated. And while Malthus was forthright in recommending plague, pestilence, and putrification, his disciples felt that the subtler and more "scientific" approaches of education, contraception, sterilization, and abortion were more practical and acceptable ways to ease the pressures of the supposed overpopulation.

The dumb certainties of experience have time and again disproved virtually every aspect of the Malthu-

sian analysis, but that proved to be little impediment
to the motley band of progressives who embraced its
idealistic notions—and who still do. As historian Paul
Johnson has shown, the Malthusians "were not men of
action." Instead, "They tried to solve the problems of
the world in the quiet of their studies, inside their
own heads . . . They produced a new vocabulary of
mumbo jumbo. It was all hard-headed, scientific, and
relentless."[3]

Even so, their doctrines were immensely appealing
to the intelligentsia and the kulturistas of the mod flap-
per set. According to Johnson:

> All the ablest elements in Western society,
> the trendsetters in opinion, were wholly
> taken in by this monstrous doctrine of
> unreason. Those who objected were success-
> fully denounced as obscurantists and the
> enemies of social progress. They could no
> longer be burned as heretical subverters of
> the new orthodoxy, but they were success-
> fully and progressively excluded from the
> control of events.[4]

They maintained an admirable don't-confuse-me-
with-the-facts aplomb when faced with the utter fan-
tasy of their scientific assumptions.

Not surprisingly, Margaret immediately got on
the Malthusian bandwagon. She was not philosophi-
cally inclined, nor was she particularly adept at political, social, or economic theory, but she did recognize
in the Malthusians a kindred spirit and a tremendous
opportunity. She was also shrewd enough to realize
that her notions of radical socialism and sexual lib-

eration would never have the popular support necessary to usher in the revolution without some appeal to altruism and intellectualism. She needed somehow to capture the moral and academic "high ground."

Malthusianism, she thought, just might be the key to that ethical and intellectual posture. If she could argue for birth control using the scientifically verified threat of poverty, sickness, racial tension, and overpopulation as its backdrop, then she would have a much better chance of making her case. So she began to absorb as much of the Malthusian dogma as she could.

Margaret also immersed herself in the teachings of each of the Malthusian offshoots. If a little bit of something is a good thing, then a lot is even better. There was Phrenology, Binetism, and Craniometricism. There was Oneidianism, Polygenesis, Recapitulationism, Lambrosianism, Hereditarianism, Freudianism, and Neotenism. From each group she picked up a few popular slogans and concepts that would permanently shape her crusade. But it was Eugenics that left the most lasting impression on the malleable mold of her nascent worldview of radicalism.

Eugenics was perhaps the most revolutionary of the pseudosciences spawned by Malthusianism. Having convinced an entire generation of scientists, intellectuals, and social reformers that the world was facing an imminent economic crisis caused by unchecked human fertility, Malthusian thought quickly turned to practical programs and social policies.

Some of these managerial Malthusians believed that the solution to the imminent crisis was political:

restrict immigration, reform social welfare, and tighten citizenship requirements. Others thought the solution was technological: increase agricultural production, improve medical proficiency, and promote industrial efficiency. But many of the rest felt that the solution was genetic: restrict or eliminate "bad racial stocks" and gradually "help to engineer the evolutionary ascent of man."

This last group became the adherents of a malevolent new voodoo-science called Eugenics. They quickly became the most influential and powerful of all the insurgent ideologists striving to rule the affairs of men and nations. In fact, for the rest of the twentieth century, they would unleash one plague after another—a whole plethora of designer disasters—upon the unsuspecting human race.

The Eugenicists unashamedly espoused an elitist White Supremacy. Or, to be more precise, they espoused an elitist Northern and Western European White Supremacy. It was not a supremacy based on the crass ethnic racism of the past but upon a new kind of "scientific" elitism deemed necessary to preserve "the best of the human race" in the face of impending doom. It was a very refined sort of supremacy that prided itself on rationalism, intellectualism, and progressivism.

This racial supremacy, they believed, had to be promoted both positively and negatively.

Through selective breeding, the Eugenicists hoped to purify the bloodlines and improve the stock of the "superior" Aryan race. The "fit" would be encouraged to reproduce prolifically. This was the positive side of Malthusian Eugenics.

Negative Malthusian Eugenics, on the other hand, sought to contain the "inferior" races through segregation, sterilization, birth control, and abortion. The "unfit" would thus be slowly winnowed out of the population as chaff is from wheat.

By the first two decades of this century, according to feminist author Germaine Greer, "The relevance of Eugenic considerations was accepted by all shades of liberal and radical opinion, as well as by many conservatives."[5]

Some forty states had enacted restrictive containment measures and established Eugenic asylums. Eugenics departments were endowed at many of the most prestigious universities in the world including Harvard, Princeton, Columbia, and Stanford. Funding for Eugenic research was provided by the Rockefeller, Ford, and Carnegie Foundations. And Eugenic ideas were given free reign in the literature, theater, music, and press of the day.[6]

The crassest sort of prejudicial class bigotry was thus embraced against the bosom of pop culture as readily and enthusiastically as the newest movie release from Hollywood or the latest hit tune from Broadway. It became a part of the collective social consciousness. Its assumptions went almost entirely unquestioned. Because it sprang full-grown from the sacrosanct temple of science—like Aphrodite on the crest of the sea or Athena from the brow of Zeus—it was placed in the modern pantheon of "truth" and rendered due faith and service by all "reasonable men."[7]

Of course, not all men are "reasonable," and so, quite thankfully, Malthusian Eugenics was not without its share of critics. The great Christian apologist G. K. Chesterton, for example, fired unrelenting salvos of biting analysis against the Eugenicists, indicting them for combining "a hardening of the heart with a sympathetic softening of the head," and for presuming to turn "common decency" and "commendable deeds" into "asocial crimes."[8] If Darwinism was the doctrine of "the survival of the fittest," he said, then Eugenics was the doctrine of "the survival of the nastiest."[9]

In his remarkably visionary book *Eugenics and Other Evils*, Chesterton pointed out, for the first time, the link between Neo-Malthusian Eugenics and the evolution of Prussian and Volkish Monism into Fascist Nazism. "It is the same stuffy science," he argued, "the same bullying bureaucracy, and the same terrorism by tenth-rate professors, that has led the German Empire to its recent conspicuous triumphs."[10]

But singular voices like Chesterton's were soon drowned out by the din of acceptance. Eugenics was the progenitor of political correctness. Long latent biases heretofore held at bay by moral convention were suddenly liberated by "science." Men were now justified in indulging their petty prejudices. And they took perverse pleasure in it, as all fallen men are wont to do.

Keen as she was to remain on the cutting edge of the *haute kultursmog*, Margaret readily embraced the racist aims and ambitions of Eugenic elitism. She was at the forefront of the fad. And it was to shape all that she was to do and all that she was to be in the momentous years that followed.

Part IV

The End of Man

"The whole point of the Eugenic pseudo-scientific theories is that they are to be applied wholesale, by some more sweeping and generalizing money power than the individual husband or wife or household. Eugenics asserts that all men must be so stupid that they cannot manage their own affairs; and also so clever that they can manage each other's."

G. K. Chesterton[1]

7

SEX EDUCATION

"Mankind declares this with one deafening voice: that sex may be ecstatic so long as it is also restricted. That is the beginning of all purity; and purity is the beginning of all passion."

G. K. Chesterton[2]

AS IMPORTANT AS HER Malthusian institutional and intellectual connections were in shaping her destiny, Margaret's English exile gave her the opportunity to make critical interpersonal connections that were more important still. Her bed became a veritable meeting place for the Fabian upper crust: H. G. Wells, George Bernard Shaw, Arnold Bennett, Arbuthnot Lane, and Norman Haire. Free from what she considered "the smothering restrictions of marital fidelity," she indulged in a nymphomaniacal passion for promiscuity and perversion.

Not satisfied even with this kind of extreme lasciviousness, she also began an unusual and tempestu-
ous affair with Havelock Ellis.

Ellis was the iconoclastic grandfather of the Bohemian sexual revolution. The author of nearly fifty
books on every aspect of concupiscence from sexual
inversion to autoeroticism, from the revolution of
obscenity to the mechanism of detumescence, from
sexual periodicity to pornographic eonism, he had provided the free love movement with much of its intellectual apologia.

Much to his chagrin, however, he himself was
sexually impotent. Thus, he spent his life in pursuit
of new and ever more exotic sensual pleasures. He
staged elaborate orgies for his Malthusian and Eugen-
icist friends; he enticed his wife into innumerable
lesbian affairs while he luridly observed in a nearby
closet; he experimented with mescaline and various
other psychotropic and psychedelic drugs; and he
established an underground network for both homo-
sexual and heterosexual extemporaneous encoun-
ters.

To Margaret, Ellis was a modern-day saint. She
adored him at once, both for his radical ideas and for
his unusual bedroom behavior. Their antics are beyond
the pale of decent discussion and somehow manage to
transcend the descriptive capacities of pedestrian
prose. They are best left unexamined.[3]

But the inculcation of animal instinct was not the
only perversity they conjured together. The two of them
began to plot a strategy for Margaret's cause. Ellis
emphasized the necessity of political expediency—he
believed that she needed to return soon to New York in

some sort of triumphant display of *faux* courage and leadership. But that would mean a few public relations adjustments. Margaret would have to tone down her rabid proabortion stance, of course. And she would have to take charge of her children once again—as distasteful as that chore would be for her—in an effort to rehabilitate her image. She would also, Ellis said, have to distance herself from revolutionary rhetoric. The scientific and philanthropic-sounding themes of Malthus and Eugenics would have to replace the politically charged themes of old-line labor Anarchism and Socialism.

By the time her year in England was over, Margaret's ideas were firmly in place, her strategy was thoroughly mapped out, and her agenda was carefully outlined. She set out for America with a demonic determination to alter the course of Western civilization. Ultimately, she would succeed—but the course she and Ellis designed was not without its high hurdles.

Margaret's first task after crossing the Atlantic, of course, was to face up to the year-old legal charges that were still outstanding against her. Using the skills she had long before developed in the IWW protests and labor strikes, she launched a brilliant public relations campaign. It rallied public support for her cause so well that authorities were forced to drop all charges.

She had won her first victory.

Then, in order to capitalize on all the publicity that her victory had generated, she embarked on a three-and-a-half-month, coast-to-coast speaking tour. She was a stunning success, drawing large, enthusiastic crowds and garnering controversial press coverage everywhere she went.

Another victory.

Next, she decided to open an illegal, back-alley birth control clinic. Papers, pamphlets, and speeches could only do so much to usher in the revolution. Following her Malthusian and Eugenic instincts, she opened her clinic in the Brownsville section of New York, an area populated by newly immigrated Slavs, Latins, Italians, and Jews. She targeted the "unfit" for her crusade to "save the planet."[4]

But there would be no victory for Margaret Sanger in this venture. Within two weeks the clinic had been shut down by authorities. Margaret and her sister, Ethel, were arrested and sentenced to thirty days each in the workhouse for the distribution of obscene materials and the prescription of dangerous contraband and deleterious medical procedures.

Predictably, Margaret was undeterred. As soon as she was released, she founded a new organization, the Birth Control League, and began to publish a new magazine, *The Birth Control Review*. She was still intent on opening a clinic, but her time in jail had convinced her that she needed to cultivate a broader following before she made another attempt. She thought that perhaps the new organization and magazine would help her do just that. And she was right—the organization and the magazine were the inauspicious beginnings of the international empire she would later dub with the innocuous-sounding moniker Planned Parenthood.

Though she was now drawing severe public criticism from such men as the fiery and popular evangelist Billy Sunday, the famed Catholic social reformer John Ryan, and the gallant former president Theodore Roosevelt, Margaret was gaining stature among the urbane and urban intelligentsia. Money poured into her office as subscriptions and donations soared. And the fact that articles from influential authors such as H. G. Wells, Pearl Buck, Julian Huxley, Karl Menninger, Havelock Ellis, and Harry Emmerson Fosdick appeared on the pages of the *Review* only boosted Margaret's topsy-turvy respectability that much more.

By 1922 her fame and fortune were unshakably secure. She had won several key legal battles, had coordinated an international conference on birth control, and had gone on a very successful round-the-world lecture tour. Her name was quickly becoming a household word and one of her numerous books had become an instant best-seller in spite of—or perhaps because of—the tremendous controversy it had caused. Entitled *The Pivot of Civilization*, it was one of the first popularly written books to openly expound and extol Malthusian and Eugenic aims. Throughout its verbose 284 pages, Margaret unashamedly called for the elimination of "human weeds," for the "cessation of charity," for the segregation of "morons, misfits, and the maladjusted," and for the sterilization of "genetically inferior races."[5]

In one passage, she followed the Malthusian party line advocating the abandonment of all forms of charity and compassion. She wrote:

> Even if we accept organized charity at its own valuation, and grant it does the best it can, it is exposed to a more profound criticism. It reveals a fundamental and irremediable defect. Its very success, its very efficiency, its very necessity to the social order are the most unanswerable indictment. Organized charity is the symptom of a malignant social disease. Those vast, com-

plex, interrelated organizations aiming to control and to diminish the spread of misery and
destitution and all the menacing evils that
spring out of this sinisterly fertile soil, are the
surest sign that our civilization has bred, is
breeding, and is perpetuating constantly
increasing numbers of defectives, delinquents,
and dependents. My criticism, therefore, is not
directed at the failure of philanthropy, but rather
at its success. These dangers inherent in the
very idea of humanitarianism and altruism,
dangers which have today produced their full
harvest of human waste.[6]

Again, she wrote:

The most serious charge that can be brought
against modern benevolence is that it encourages the perpetuation of defectives, delinquents, and dependents. These are the most
dangerous elements in the world community,
the most devastating curse on human progress
and expression. Philanthropy is a gesture
characteristic of modern business lavishing
upon the unfit the profits extorted from the
community at large. Looked at impartially,
this compensatory generosity is in its final
effect probably more dangerous, more dysgenic, more blighting than the initial practice
of profiteering.[7]

Published today, such a book would be immediately labeled as abominably racist and totalitarian. But
writing when she did, Margaret only gained more
acclaim. It was, after all, the heyday of Socialism and

its ideological kissing cousin, Fascism.

Paradoxically, her cause seemed all but unstoppable now. Margaret's great social revolution had truly begun.

8

HUMAN WEEDS

"We are not so very far off from even the sacrifice of babies—if not to a crocodile, at least to a creed."

G. K. Chesterton[1]

PLANNED PARENTHOOD OFFICIALS HAVE always tried to deflect any criticism of their founder's radical and racist worldview. Though they have managed all manner of epistemological gymnastics and historical revisionism in a feeble attempt to deny it, hide it, and belie it, Margaret was undeniably mesmerized by the fashionable elitism of Malthusian Eugenics.[2]

Part of the attraction for her was, obviously, political: virtually all of her Socialist friends, lovers, and comrades were committed Eugenicists—from the followers of Lenin in Revolutionary Socialism, like H. G. Wells, George Bernard Shaw, and Julius Hammer, to the followers of Hitler in National Socialism, like Ernest Rudin, Leon Whitney, and Harry Laughlin.

And part of the attraction for her was also personal: her mentor and lover, Havelock Ellis, was the beloved disciple of Francis Galton, the brilliant cousin of Charles Darwin who first systemized and popularized Eugenic thought.

But it wasn't simply politics or sentiment that drew Margaret into the Eugenic fold. She was thoroughly convinced that the "inferior races" were in fact "human weeds" and a "menace to civilization." She really believed that "social regeneration" would only be possible as the "sinister forces of the hordes of irresponsibility and imbecility" were repulsed. She had come to regard organized charity to ethnic minorities and the poor as a "symptom of a malignant social disease" because it encouraged the prolificacy of those "defectives, delinquents, and dependents" she so obviously abhorred. She yearned for the end of the Christian "reign of benevolence" that the Eugenic Socialists promised, when the "choking human undergrowth" of "morons and imbeciles" would be "segregated" and ultimately "sterilized." Her greatest aspiration was "to create a race of thoroughbreds" by encouraging "more children from the fit, and less from the unfit." And the only way to achieve that dystopic goal, she realized, was through the harsh and coercive tyranny of Malthusian Eugenics.[3]

In other words, she was a true believer, not simply someone who assimilated the jargon of the times—as Planned Parenthood officials would have us believe. She was a committed elitist bent on undermining the familial bonds of the poor and disenfranchised.[4]

As she began to build the work of the American Birth Control League and, ultimately, of Planned Parenthood, Margaret relied heavily on the men, women, ideas, and resources of the Eugenics movement. Virtually all of the organization's board members were Eugenicists. Financing for the early projects—from the opening of the first birth control clinics to the publishing of the revolutionary literature—came from Eugenicists. The speakers at the conferences, the authors of the propaganda, and the providers of the services were almost without exception avid Eugenicists. And as if that rather substantial evidence was not enough, the international work of Planned Parenthood was originally housed in the offices of the Eugenics Society—while the organizations themselves were institutionally intertwined for years.

The Birth Control Review—Margaret's magazine and the immediate predecessor to the *Planned Parenthood Review*—regularly and openly published the racist articles of Malthusian Eugenicists. In 1920, for instance, it published a favorable review of Lothrop Stoddard's frightening book of Fascist diatribe, *The Rising Tide of Color Against White World Supremacy*. In 1923 the *Review* editorialized in favor of restricting immigration on a racial basis. In 1932 it outlined Margaret's "Plan for Peace," which called for coercive sterilization, mandatory segregation, and rehabilitative concentration camps for all "dysgenic stocks." In 1933 the *Review* published a shocking article entitled "Eugenic Sterilization: An Urgent Need." It was written by Margaret's close friend and advisor, Ernst Rudin, who was then serving as Hitler's director of genetic sterilization and had earlier taken a prominent role in the establishment of the Nazi Society for Racial Hygiene. Later that same year it published an article by Leon Whitney entitled "Selective Sterilization," which adamantly praised and defended the Third Reich's preholocaust "race purification" programs.

The bottom line is that Margaret self-consciously organized the Birth Control League—and its progeny, Planned Parenthood—in part to promote and enforce the scientifically elitist notions of White Supremacy. Like the Ku Klux Klan, the Nazi Party, and the Mensheviks, Margaret's enterprise was from its inception implicitly and explicitly racist. And this racist orientation was all too evident in its various programs and initiatives: government control over family decisions, nonmedicinal health-care experimentations, the rabid abortion crusade, and the coercive sterilization initiatives.

Margaret's first wild stab at opening a birth control clinic, for example, was strategically aimed at the impoverished and densely populated Brownsville section of Brooklyn. The ramshackle two-room, back-alley hovel was a far cry from Margaret's plush Greenwich Village haunts. But since the clientele she wished to attract, the "dysgenic immigrant Southern Europeans, Slavs, Latins, and Jews," could only be lured into her snare "in the coarser neighborhoods and tenements," she was forced to venture out of her more familiar and comfortable confines.

As her organization grew in power and prestige, she began to target several other "ill-favored" and "dysgenic races," including "Blacks, Hispanics, Amerinds, Fundamentalists, and Catholics."[5] It was not long before she set up clinics in their respective com-

munities as well. Margaret and the Malthusian Eugenicists she had gathered about her were not partial; all
non-Aryans—Red, Yellow, Black, or White—all were
noxious in their sight. They sought to place new clinics wherever those "feeble-minded, syphilitic, irresponsible, and defective" stocks "bred unhindered."
Since by their estimation as much as 70 percent of the
population fell into this "undesirable" category, Margaret and her cohorts really had their work cut out for
them.

They were more than up to the task.

In 1939 Margaret designed a "Negro Project" in
response to requests from "southern state public health
officials"—men not generally known for their racial
equanimity.[6] "The mass of Negroes," her project proposal asserted, "particularly in the South, still breed
carelessly and disastrously, with the result that the
increase among Negroes, even more than among
Whites, is from that portion of the population least
intelligent and fit." The proposal went on to say that
"Public Health statistics merely hint at the primitive
state of civilization in which most Negroes in the South
live."[7]

In order to remedy this "dysgenic horror story,"
her project aimed to hire three or four "Colored Ministers, preferably with social-service backgrounds, and
with engaging personalities," to travel to various Black
enclaves and propagandize for birth control.[8]

"The most successful educational approach to the
Negro," Margaret wrote sometime later, "is through a
religious appeal. We do not want word to go out that
we want to exterminate the Negro population, and
the Minister is the man who can straighten out that

idea if it ever occurs to any of their more rebellious members."[9]

Of course, those Black ministers were to be carefully controlled—mere figureheads. "There is a great danger that we will fail," one of the project directors wrote, "because the Negroes think it is a plan for extermination. Hence, let's appear to let the colored run it." Another project director lamented, "I wonder if Southern Darkies can ever be entrusted with . . . a clinic. Our experience causes us to doubt their ability to work except under White supervision." The entire operation then was a ruse—a manipulative attempt to get Blacks to cooperate in their own elimination.[10]

Sadly, the project was quite successful. Its genocidal intentions were carefully camouflaged beneath several layers of condescending social service rhetoric and organizational expertise. Like the citizens of Hamlin, lured into captivity by the sweet serenades of the Pied Piper, all too many Blacks across the country happily fell into step behind Margaret and the Eugenic racists she had placed on her Negro Advisory Council.

Soon clinics throughout the South were distributing contraceptives to Blacks and Margaret's dream of discouraging "the defective and diseased elements of humanity" from their "reckless and irresponsible swarming and spawning" was at last being fulfilled.

The strategy was, of course, racial and not geographical. The Southern states were picked simply because of the high proportion of Blacks in their populations. In later decades, expansion to the North and West occurred. But the basic guidelines remained: the proportion of minorities in a community was closely related to the density of birth control clinics.

The "champion of birth control" and the "patron saint of feminism" was no less horrific in her disdain for the helpless and the hapless than any of the other monsters of progressivism during the first half of the twentieth century—Hitler, Stalin, Mussolini, and Mao. The only difference is that they have all been duly discredited, while she has not—at least, not yet.

PART V

TO BE OR NOT TO BE

"What I complain of is the shallowness of people who only do things for a change and then actually talk as if the change were unchangeable. That is the weakness of a purely progressive theory. The very latest opinion is always infallibly right and always inevitably wrong."

G. K. Chesterton[1]

9

A New World Order

"Civilization is only one of the things that men choose to have. Convince them of its uselessness and they would fling away civilization as they fling away a cigar."

G. K. Chesterton[2]

In 1925 Margaret Sanger hosted an "international neo-Malthusian and birth control conference" at the tiny Hotel McAlpin in New York. She had grown increasingly concerned that societal, civic, and religious pressure might snuff out her nascent Eugenic ideals. As she asserted:

> The government of the United States deliberately encourages and even makes necessary by its laws the breeding—with a breakneck rapidity—of idiots, defectives, diseased, feeble-

minded, and criminal classes. Billions of
dollars are expended by our state and federal
governments and by private charities and philanthropies for the care, the maintenance, and
the perpetuation of these classes. Year by year
their numbers are mounting. Year by year
more money is expended . . . to maintain an
increasing race of morons which threatens the
very foundations of our civilization.[3]

She was especially distressed by the dim prospects
that democratic suffrage afforded her dystopic plans to
implement a universal system of inhuman humanism:

We can all vote, even the mentally arrested.
And so it is no surprise to find that the moron's
vote is as good as the vote of the genius. The
outlook is not a cheerful one.[4]

If there was little for her to cheer about in America,
there was even less on the international scene. Europe,
decimated by the Great War, was desperate to reverse
its dramatic decline in population. At the same time the
developing world was no less desperate to stoke the
hopeful fires of progress with aggressive population
growth. Despite the fast start of her various enterprises,
Margaret's message was falling on increasingly deaf ears.

By convening dozens of like-minded "neo-Malthusian pioneers" from around the world, she was hopeful
that together they would be able to circle the wagons, to
"develop a new evangelistic strategy," and ultimately to
reverse the tide of public opinion and public policy—
and thus "to keep alive and carry on the torch of neo-
Malthusian truth."[5]

For six days representatives from France, England,

Norway, Holland, Austria, Hungary, Germany, Belgium, Spain, Sweden, Switzerland, Italy, Portugal, India, South Africa, Russia, Mexico, Canada, Japan, and China listened as "experts" delivered papers, made speeches, held workshops, and offered dire prophesies.

They suggested new political tactics. They crafted coy public relations schemes. And they hammered out a bevy of priorities, agendas, and schedules. In addition to all that, they harked to plenary portents, admonitions, and jeremiads that:

> The dullard, the gawk, the numbskull, the simpleton, the weakling, and the scatterbrain are amongst us in overshadowing numbers— intermarrying, breeding, inordinately prolific, literally threatening to overwhelm the world with their useless and terrifying get.[6]

By the end of the conference it was apparent to all of them that unless they took "a course of drastic action the world would face certain imminent disaster." Many had been involved in some sort of subversive sex-activism for quite some time—each of the participants claimed membership in the International Federation of Neo-Malthusian Leagues, and most were leaders in the International Eugenics Society. Even so, the time for united purpose and concerted effort was clearly at hand. A loose federation of "race hygiene societies," "birth control leagues," "family planning associations," and "social Eugenics committees" was formalized. Drawing on the heritage of Annie Bessant, Charles Bradlaugh, Charles Drysdale, and Alice Vickery—all radicals and aspiring social engineers from an earlier generation—the new federation took a self-consciously

presuppositional anti-Christian, antifamily, and anti-
choice bent from the start.

The federation would not be incorporated as International Planned Parenthood until a reorganizational
meeting in Bombay shortly after the Second World
War, but, nonetheless, it remained active during the
intervening years. Sharing offices and resources with
their kith and kin in the International Eugenics Society, the members did not want to rush the careful
implementation of their strategic plan unnecessarily.
Thus, it was during that developmental period that
Margaret and the other leaders laid the philosophical
foundations that to this day characterize the organization and its multifarious programs.

They made certain, for instance, that all national
affiliates would adhere to a stridently proabortion
stance. In fact, they determined that all Planned Parenthood associations—regardless of social, cultural, or
political contexts—make "legal access" to "unrestricted
abortion" a "high priority." As Malcolm Potts, the medical director for the international federation, admitted
years later:

> The fact is, that no nation on earth has con-
> trolled its fertility without abortion. The
> United States has 1.5 million abortions a year.
> Why should we expect Indonesia, say, to do
> better? No matter how good the method is,
> you can't get adequate fertility control with
> contraception alone. You have got to grapple
> with sterilization and abortion.[7]

The federation also made sure that the national
affiliates pressed for coercive government action to

enforce birth limitations and Eugenic sterilizations. Through the imposition of legal and economic reproductive incentives and disincentives, they encouraged national organizations to weigh the necessity of "limiting freedom of choice." Suggested sanctions included the "introduction of a child tax," "reduction or elimination of paid maternity leave and benefits," "limitation or elimination of public-financed medical care, scholarships, housing loans, and subsidies to families with more than the allowed number of children," or even "compulsory sterilizations and abortions."[8]

In later years that preferential bent toward totalitarianism led Planned Parenthood to laud the brutal one-child-per-family program of the Communist Chinese as a "stunning success" that was "worth our attention and awe." They made certain that each national affiliate would develop and implement "value-free" sex-education curricula and programs. Advocating the kinds of programs that the American affiliate pioneered—using perverse off-the-shelf commercial pornography in elementary classrooms, undermining traditional values, usurping the authority of parents, and encouraging promiscuous activity—they imposed a kind of smothering ideological uniformity.

Accordingly, the international literature policy asserted:

> The broad abstract principles inspired by an antique, repressive morality serve only to confuse us . . . As hard as it is to admit sexual precocity is a fact that is present, progressive, and irreversible . . . Only those who admit, accept, and validate the possibility of an early exercise of sexuality will have placed themselves in a

condition to be able to channel it through education.[9]

Each of the federation's national affiliates were mandated to overcome legal obstacles that impeded the overarching Planned Parenthood agenda of Eugenic cleansing by using various forms of legal challenges, popular protests, and acts of civil disobedience. At times that might mean merely sidestepping the law: in the Philippines, where abortions are illegal, Planned Parenthood offers "menstrual extractions" instead—despite the fact that the procedures are, for all intents and purposes, technically the same. At other times clear violation of the law is perpetrated: in Brazil where sterilization is illegal, Planned Parenthood performs as many as twenty million of the procedures every year in its field clinics.[10]

According to one internal directive issued from the London office:

> Family Planning Associations and other non-government organizations should not use the absence of the law or the existence of an unfavorable law as an excuse for inaction; action outside the law, and even in violation of it, is part of the process of stimulating change.[11]

Though these ideas were more than a little radical, their careful presentation and prudent institutionalization—under the ever-watchful management of Margaret and the other neo-Malthusians—eventually paid off. And it paid off in huge dividends.

Ultimately, most of Planned Parenthood's neo-Malthusian ideas found their way into some of the most significant political, cultural, and social programs of the twentieth century as modern presuppositional tenets of an aggressive and universal politically correct orthodoxy. Unlikely support for the ideas sprang up everywhere. Opposition practically evaporated. Within just a few years, the revolution that Margaret had hoped for and dreamed of had become a veritable reality.

Adolf Hitler, for instance, adopted the neo-Malthusian ideas of Margaret and her friends in a wholesale fashion in his administration of the Third Reich—his exterminative "final solution," his coercive abortion program in Poland, Yugoslavia, and Czechoslovakia, and his elitist national socialism. He echoed the Malthusian call to "rid the earth of dysgenic peoples by whatever means available so that we may enjoy the prosperity of the Fatherland." And he reiterated the Planned Parenthood ideal of eliminating all Christian mercy ministries or social service programs. "Let us spend our efforts and our resources," he cried in a frenetic speech in 1939, "on the productive, not on the wastrel."

Josef Stalin also included Planned Parenthood's neo-Malthusian ideal in his brutal interpretation of Marxism—his Ukrainian triage, his collectivization of the Kulaks, and his Siberian genocide. He argued that "The greatest obstacle to the successful completion of the people's revolution is the swarming of inferior races from the south and east." And the only thing that prevented him from eliminating that obstacle was "the foolhardy interference of church charity."

The concessions to Margaret's malignant philosophy did not end there. Before long, the Planned Parenthood planners and prognosticators were riding a

tidal wave of success as one political system after
another capitulated to the intolerant demands of
Eugenicism:

> • In 1938 Sweden became the first free
> nation in Christendom to revert to pre-
> Christian abortion legislation and to
> institutionalize Planned Parenthood's
> sex-education and family limitation pro-
> grams.

> • Between 1949 and 1956 abortion was
> legalized in eleven more European
> nations—each at the behest of Planned
> Parenthood.

> • In 1954 Planned Parenthood held an
> international conference on abortion and
> called for "reform" of restrictive legislation.

> • In 1958 various United Nations agencies
> began to subsidize Planned Parenthood
> projects and programs throughout the
> developing world.

> • In 1962 the American Law Institute pro-
> posed that abortion laws be decriminalized.

> • In 1967 the American Medical Associa-
> tion reversed its century-old commitment
> to protect the lives of the unborn, and it
> began calling for decriminalization and
> destigmatization of abortion.

> • Also in 1967 three states—Colorado,
> California, and North Carolina—loos-
> ened restrictions on certain child-killing

procedures.

• In 1968 the United Kingdom legalized abortion.

• Later in 1968, Pope Paul VI issued his *Humanae Vitae* encyclical which, among other things, reaffirmed the Church's commitment to the sanctity of life. Since this seemed to be the lone Christian voice of dissent during a massive juggernaut of neo-pagan revivalism, the abortion issue quickly came to be viewed in the public arena as a Catholic issue.

• In 1970 four more states—Hawaii, Alaska, Washington, and New York— enacted abortion-on-demand legislation.

• By the end of 1971, nearly half a million legal abortions were being performed in the United States each year and another two million worldwide.

• Then in 1973 the Supreme Court issued its momentous *Roe v. Wade* decree that altered the moral landscape of modern America in a single act of sheer judicial fiat—thus signaling a keen message of relativism to the rest of the world.

And from there, things have only gone from bad to worse. Taking full advantage of its newfound global consensus, Planned Parenthood has launched a massive campaign to construct a New World Order in accord with Margaret's original revolutionary design.

As unlikely as it seemed when she first began her lurid campaign, Margaret had succeeded—with a vengeance.

10

The
Marrying Kind

"The wisdom of man alters with every age; his prudence has to fit perpetually shifting shapes of inconvenience or dilemma. But his folly is immortal: a fire stolen from heaven."

G. K. Chesterton[1]

D ESPITE HER STUNNING SUCCESS, by 1922 Margaret was miserable. Her private life was in utter shambles. Her marriage, of course, had ended long ago. During one of Margaret's many long absences, her daughter, Peggy, caught cold and died of pneumonia. Her boys were neglected and forgotten. And her once-ravishing beauty was fading with age and self-abuse.

Desperate to find meaning and happiness, she lost herself in a profusion of sexual liaisons. She went from one lover to another, sometimes several in a single day. She experimented with innumerable erotic fantasies and fetishes, but satisfaction always eluded her grasp. She began to dabble in the occult, participating in séances and practicing Eastern meditation. She even went so far as to apply for initiation into the mysteries of Rosicrucianism and Theosophy.

When all else failed, she turned to the one thing that she knew would bring her solace: once again, she married into money.

J. Noah Slee was the president of the Three-in-One Oil Company and a legitimate millionaire. A conservative churchgoing Episcopalian, he opposed everything that Margaret stood for, but found her irresistible anyway.

At first, Margaret resisted his pleas for marriage. She still believed that it was a "degenerate institution." But $9 million was a mighty temptation. It was a temptation she simply could not resist.

To make certain that the new relationship would not interfere with her sordid affairs and her vicious cause, she drew up a prenuptial agreement that Slee was forced to sign just before the wedding ceremony. It stipulated that Margaret would be free to come and go as she pleased, no questions asked. She would have her own apartment and servants within her husband's home, where she could entertain "friends" of her own choosing—behind closed doors. Furthermore, Slee would have to telephone her from the other end of the house to even ask for a dinner date.

Margaret told her lovers that her marriage to Slee would make little or no difference in her life—apart from the convenience of the money, of course. And she went out of her way to prove it; she flaunted her promiscuity and infidelity every chance she could get.

She was still terribly unhappy, but at least now she was terribly rich, too.

Immediately, Margaret committed herself to using her new wealth to further the cause. She opened a new clinic—this time calling it a "Research Bureau" in order to avoid legal tangles. Then she began to smuggle diaphragms into the country from Holland. She waged several successful "turf" battles to maintain control over her "empire." She campaigned diligently to win over the medical community. She secured massive foundation grants from the Rockefellers, the Fords, and the Mellons. She took her struggle to Washington, testifying before several congressional committees, advocating the liberalization of contraceptive prescription laws. And she fought for the incorporation of reproductive control into state programs as a form of social planning. With her almost unlimited financial resources, she was able to open doors and pull strings that had heretofore been entirely inaccessible to her.

Margaret was also able to use her newfound wealth to fight an important public relations campaign to redeem her reputation—which despite her success bore the taint of radicalism and social disruption.

Because of her Malthusian and Eugenic connections, she had willingly become closely associated with the scientists and theorists who put together Nazi Germany's "race purification" program. She had openly endorsed the euthanasia, sterilization, abortion, and infanticide programs of the early Reich. She happily published a number of articles in *The Birth Control Review* that mirrored Hitler's Aryan-White Supremacist rhetoric. She even commissioned her friend, Ernst

Rudin, director of the Nazi Medical Experimentation program, to serve the organization as an advisor.

Naturally, when World War II broke out and grisly details of Nazi programs were exposed, Margaret was forced to backpedal her position and cover up her complicity. The Great Depression had been a boon for racist and Eugenic arguments, but those days were gone. Charges of anti-Semitism had been harmlessly hurled at her since her trial in 1917, but now that Auschwitz and Dachau were very much a part of the public conscience, she realized she would have to do something, and do it quickly.

Her first step toward redeeming her public image was to change the name of her organization. "Planned Parenthood" was a name that had been proposed from within the birth control movement since at least 1938. One of the arguments for the new name was that it connoted a positive program and conveyed a clean, wholesome, family-oriented image. It diverted attention from the international and revolutionary Eugenic intentions of the movement, focusing instead on the personal and individual dimensions of birth control. By 1942 the decision had been made. The organization would be called the Planned Parenthood Federation of America.

Next, she embarked on an aggressive affiliation program that brought hundreds of local and regional birth control leagues under the umbrella of a national organization, and then dozens of national organizations were brought under the umbrella of an international organization. This enabled Margaret to draw on the integrity and respectability of grassroots organizations, solidifying and securing her place at the top.

Finally, she initiated a massive propaganda blitz aimed at the war-weary, ready-for-prosperity middle class. Always careful to hide her illicit affairs and her radical political leanings, Margaret effected a campaign that emphasized patriotism, personal choice, and family values.

Before long, Margaret's brilliant strategy had won for her, and Planned Parenthood, the admiration and respect of virtually the entire nation, and certainly of the entire social services community.

It is said that it takes money to make money. Soon, Margaret was able to prove the veracity of this truism.

From its earliest days, Planned Parenthood wooed corporations, foundations, celebrities, and charities in the hope of securing operating capital. With her newly minted respectability—bought with Slee's bottomless coffers—Margaret was able to open the treasury of American corporate philanthropy in an unprecedented fashion.

She rubbed shoulders and shared beds with the radical chic throughout the Roaring Twenties—the artists, actors, writers, musicians, and activists in New York's chic Village and London's mod Fabian Enclave. She shrewdly used her proximity to them to promote her revolutionary ideas. And she carefully networked with them to gain contacts in the political and financial world.

Single-minded in her commitment to *the cause*, Margaret used persistence and unflagging enthusiasm to open doors. She was tireless and driven. Some even said she was "possessed"—which, no doubt, she was. At any rate, her crusade quickly became a cause célèbre. By the thirties corporation grants and foundation bequests began to pour money into her war chest. By

the forties she had won the endorsements of such nota-
bles as Eleanor Roosevelt and Katharine Hepburn. By
the fifties she had attained international renown and
counted among her supporters Julian Huxley, Albert
Einstein, Nehru, John D. Rockefeller, Emperor Hiro-
hito, and Henry Ford. The sixties brought her tremendous fame and acceptance. Before her death she
received the enthusiastic endorsements of former presi-
dents Harry Truman and Dwight Eisenhower. She won
over archconservatives like Barry Goldwater, and arch-
liberals like Margaret Mead. Ideology didn't seem to
matter.[2]

On top of all this Margaret Sanger was a tenacious
organizer. Her days with the Socialist Party and the
Communist Labor movement not only trained her in
effective propaganda techniques, they taught her how
to solicit, train, and activate volunteers. Using these
skills, Margaret literally combed the country and, ultimately, the world searching for donors. She left no
stone unturned. She applied for every grant, appealed
to every foundation, made presentations to every corporation, and appealed to every charity. She wanted a
piece of every philanthropic pie, and she went to great
pains to make her case to anyone who would listen.
She was a dogged promoter. And, like the persistent
widow in Christ's parable, she was so unrelenting, she
prevailed more times than not (Luke 18:1-8).

Perhaps Margaret's greatest coup came when she
was able to gain IRS charitable tax-exempt status for
her organization. That put Planned Parenthood in the
same legal category as a local church or a philanthropic
society. All donations became tax-deductible, and that
made solicitation and donor development all the easier.

The fund-raising apparatus that she established has only grown in size and sophistication in the years since her death. It has garnered hundreds of celebrity endorsements. It has affiliated with every major national and international professional and educational association even remotely related to Planned Parenthood's work. And it has tapped into the fiscal lifeblood of virtually every major charitable resource available.

Of course, these tremendous successes did little to ease the ache of Margaret's perpetual unhappiness. She continued her sordid and promiscuous affairs even after old age and poor health had overtaken her. Her pathetic attraction to occultism deepened. Perhaps worst of all, by 1949 she had become addicted to both drugs and alcohol.

That improvidence was almost her undoing.

From its earliest days the Planned Parenthood movement had been involved in financial scandal. Despite the fact that she received generous donations from some of the richest philanthropies in the world, Margaret kept her organization on the brink of bankruptcy for years, failing to pay her bills and refusing to give an account of her mismanagement.[3]

Financial disclosure would certainly have brought disaster upon her—as well as upon her fledgling operation. She often spent Planned Parenthood money for her own extravagant pleasures. She invested organizational funds in the black market. She squandered hard-won bequests on frivolities. And she wasted the money she'd gotten "by hook or by crook" on her unrestrained vanities.

Because of her wastrel indiscretions, Margaret was quietly removed from the Planned Parenthood board several times, but the organization found that it simply could not survive without her. In the end Planned Parenthood was forced to take on the character and attributes of its founder. "The love of money is the root of all evil" (1 Timothy 6:10). Violence and greed are inseparable (Proverbs 1:8-19). Thus, Planned Parenthood's evil agenda of violence to women and children cannot be cut loose from the deep taproot of avarice and material lust that Margaret planted.

Sexual immorality, theft, adultery, covetousness, greed, malice, wickedness, deceit, lewdness, lasciviousness, arrogance, blasphemy, pride, ruthlessness, and folly are all related sins (Mark 7:21-22). They commonly coexist (Romans 1:29-31). They certainly did in the tortured concupiscence of Margaret Sanger. And they still do, in the organization that honors her as a pioneer and champion.

By the time she died on September 6, 1966, a week shy of her eighty-seventh birthday, Margaret Sanger had nearly fulfilled her early boast that she would spend every last penny of Slee's fortune. In the process, though, she had lost everything else: love, happiness, satisfaction, fulfillment, family, and friends. In the end, her struggle was for naught.

"For what does it profit a man to gain the whole world, but to lose his own soul? Or what shall a man give in exchange for his soul?" (Mark 8:36-37).

PART VI

HOW SHOULD WE THEN LIVE?

"The business of progressives is to keep on making mistakes. The business of conservatives is to prevent the mistakes being corrected. Even when the revolutionist might himself repent of his revolution, the traditionalist is already defending it as a part of his tradition. Thus we have the two great types—the advanced person who rushes us to ruin, and the retrospective person who admires the ruins."

G. K. Chesterton[1]

11

Root and Fruit

"The advantage of being a sentimentalist is that you only remember what you like to remember."

G. K. Chesterton[2]

J UST AS A NATION'S "head" defines the character and vision of that nation, so an organization's "head" defines the character and vision of that organization.

This is a very basic Biblical principle. It is the principle of "legacy." It is the principle of "inheritance."

The Canaanite people were perverse and corrupt. They practiced every manner of wickedness and reprobation. Why were they so dissolute? The answer, according to the Bible, is that their founders and leaders passed evil onto them as their *legacy*, as their *inheritance* (Genesis 9:25; Leviticus 18:24-25; Amos 1:3-12).

Similarly, the Moabites and the Ammonites were a rebellious and improvident people. They railed against God's Word and God's People. Why were they so defiant? Again, the Bible tells us that their founders and leaders passed insurrection on to them as their *legacy*, as their *inheritance* (Genesis 19:30-38; Numbers 21:21-23; Amos 1:13-15; Amos 2:1-3).

A seed will always yield its own kind (Genesis 1:11). Bad seed brings forth bitter harvest (Ezra 9:2; Isaiah 1:4; Isaiah 14:20). You reap what you sow (Galatians 6:7). A nation or an organization that is sown, nurtured, and grown by deceit, promiscuity, and lawlessness, cannot help but be evil to the core (Hosea 8:7).

Planned Parenthood is a paradigmatical illustration of these principles. Margaret Sanger's character and vision are perfectly mirrored in the organization that she wrought. She intended it that way. And the leaders that have come after her have in no way attempted to have it any other way.

Dr. Alan Guttmacher, the man who immediately succeeded her as president of Planned Parenthood Federation of America, once said, "We are merely walking down the path that Mrs. Sanger carved out for us." Faye Wattleton, president of the organization during the decade of the eighties, claimed that she is "proud" to be "walking in the footsteps of Margaret Sanger." And the president of the New York affiliate is Alexander Sanger, her grandson.[3]

Thus, virtually everything that Margaret believed, everything that she aspired to, everything that she practiced, and everything that she aimed for is somehow reflected in the organization and program of Planned Parenthood, even today. The frightening thing about Planned Parenthood's historical legacy is that the legacy is not just historical. It is as current as tomorrow morning's newspaper.

Abortion. In her book *Women and the New Race*, Margaret asserted that "The most merciful thing a large family can do to one of its infant members is to kill it."[4] Today, Planned Parenthood's commitment to that philosophy is self-evident. The organization is the world's number-one abortion provider and agitator. It has aggressively fought the issue through the courts. It has made killing infant members of large families its highest priority. Bad seed brings forth bitter harvest. The legacy continues.

Promiscuity. Like her mentors Emma Goldman and Havelock Ellis, Margaret was not content to keep her lascivious and concupiscent behavior to herself. She was a zealous evangelist for free love. Even in her old age, she persisted in proselytizing to her sixteen-year-old granddaughter, telling her that kissing, petting, and even intercourse were fine as long as she was "sincere," and that having sex about "three times a day" was "just about right."[5] Today, Planned Parenthood's commitment to undermining the moral values of teens is evident in virtually all its literature. It teaches kids to masturbate. It endorses premarital fornication. It approves of homosexuality. It encourages sexual experimentation. It vilifies Christian values, prohibitions, and consciences. Bad seed brings forth bitter harvest. The legacy continues.

Socialism. Margaret Sanger was committed to the revolution. She wanted to overthrow the old order of Western Christendom and usher in a "New Age." Though in her later years she toned down her radical rhetoric, she never wavered from that stance. Today, Planned Parenthood continues to carry the banner for big government, big spending, and freewheeling liberal causes and agendas. Even the normally sedate *Wall Street Journal* had to admit that "Planned Parenthood's love affair with Socialism has become more than a harmless upper middle-class hobby and now borders on the ludicrous."[6] Bad seed brings forth bitter harvest. The legacy continues.

Greed. When Leon Trotsky briefly visited the United States in 1917, he met Margaret and her friends, and he came away with a feeling of great revulsion. In his memoirs he recorded nothing but distaste for the rich, smug Socialists he encountered in the Village. He said they were little better than "hypocritical Babbits," referring to the Sinclair Lewis character who used his parlor-room Socialism as a screen for personal ambition and self-aggrandizement.[7] Margaret and the other Village elitists were revolutionaries only to the extent that Socialism did not conflict with wealth, luxury, and political influence. Today, Planned Parenthood's commitment to the revolution continues to hinge on that unswerving pursuit of "filthy lucre." From its dogged preoccupation with government contracts, grants, and bequests, to its commercial ventures, investments, and vocations, its mercenary avariciousness is apparent everywhere. Bad seed brings forth bitter harvest. The legacy continues.

Religion. In her first newspaper, *The Woman Rebel,* Margaret Sanger admitted that "Birth control appeals to the advanced radical because it is calculated to undermine the authority of the Christian churches. I look forward to seeing humanity free someday of the

tyranny of Christianity no less than Capitalism."[8]
Today, Planned Parenthood is continuing her crusade
against the Church. In its advertisements, in its literature, in its programs, and in its policies, the organization makes every attempt to mock, belittle, and
undermine Biblical Christianity. Bad seed brings forth
bitter harvest. The legacy continues.

Deceit. Throughout her life, Margaret Sanger developed a rakish and reckless pattern of dishonesty. She
twisted the truth about her qualifications as a nurse,
about the details of her work, and about the various
sordid addictions that controlled her life. Her autobiog-
raphies were filled with exaggerations, distortions, and
out-and-out lies. She even went so far as to alter the
records in her mother's family Bible in order to protect
her vanity. Today, Planned Parenthood faithfully carries
on her tradition of disinformation. The organization con-
tinually misrepresents the facts about its lucrative birth
control, sex education, and abortion enterprises. Bad
seed brings forth bitter harvest. The legacy continues.

A recent Planned Parenthood report bore the
slogan "Proud of Our Past—Planning the Future."[9] If
that is true—if the organization really is proud of its
venal and profligate past, and if it really is planning the
future—then we all have much to be concerned about.

"Those who plow iniquity and those who sow trou-
ble harvest it. By the breath of God they perish, and by
the blast of His anger they come to an end."(Job 4:8-9).

12

THE BIG LIE

"The new myth is generally a part of a new theory; not a confused remembrance, but a conscious reconstruction."

G. K. Chesterton[1]

THEY SAY THAT SHE was "enlightened." They say she was "compassionate." They say she was a "champion of freedom." They say she was concerned "first and foremost with the needs of the needy and the wants of the wanting."[2]

Lies. Lies. Lies. All lies.

One after another, the hagiographical lies of Margaret's faithful and fawning followers in Planned Parenthood, hallowed in near sanctity, blaze forth in a positive conflagration of revered shibboleths. Taken

116

together, those lies comprise the lie. The Big Lie. The Grand Illusion. The Modern Myth.

Myths, according to theologian J. I. Packer, are "stories made up to sanctify social patterns.[3] They are lies, carefully designed to reinforce a particular philosophy or morality within a culture. They are instruments of manipulation and control."

When Jeroboam splintered the nation of Israel after the death of Solomon, he thought that in order to consolidate his rule over the northern faction he would have to wean the people from their spiritual and emotional dependence on the Jerusalem temple. So he manufactured myths. He lied.

> And Jeroboam said in his heart, 'Now the kingdom will return to the house of David. If this people go up to offer sacrifices in the house of the Lord at Jerusalem, then the heart of this people will return to their lord, even to Rehoboam king of Judah; and they will kill me and return to Rehoboam king of Judah.' So the king consulted, and made two golden calves, and he said to them, 'It is too much for you to go up to Jerusalem; behold your gods, O Israel, that brought you up from the land of Egypt.' And he set one in Bethel, and the other he put in Dan. Now this thing became a sin, for the people went to worship before the one as far as Dan. And he made houses on high places, and made priests from among all the people who were not of the sons of Levi. And Jeroboam instituted a feast in the eighth month on the fifteenth day of the month, like the feast which is in Judah, and he went up to the altar; thus he did in Bethel, sacrificing to the calves which

> he had made. And he stationed in Bethel the
> priests of the high places which he had made.
> Then he went up to the altar which he had
> made in Bethel on the fifteenth day in the
> eighth month, even in the month which he
> had devised in his own heart; and he instituted
> a feast for the sons of Israel, and went up to
> the altar to burn incense (1 Kings 12:26-33).

Jeroboam instituted a false feast at a false shrine,
attended by false priests, before false gods, and he did
all this on a false pretense. But his lies succeeded in
swaying the people. Jeroboam's mythology sanctified
a whole new set of social patterns. What would have
been unthinkable before—idolatry, apostasy, and
travesty—became almost overnight not only think-
able or acceptable, but conventional and habitual. As
a result, the new king was able to manipulate and
control his subjects.

The powerful, the would-be-powerful, and the
wish-they-were-powerful have always relied on such
tactics. Plato and Thucydides observed the phenome-
non during Greece's classical era. Plutarch and Augus-
tine identified it during the Roman epoch. Sergios
Kasilov and Basil Argyros noted it during the Byzan-
tine millennium. Niccolo Machiavelli and Thomas
More recognized its importance during the European
Renaissance. And Aleksandr Solzhenitsyn and Colin
Thubron have pointed it out in our own time.

Most of the mythmakers never actually believed in
the gods upon Olympus, across the River Styx, or
within the Kremlin Palace. After all, they knew all too
well from whence those lies came. But as high priests
of deceit, they used the lies to dominate the hearts and

minds and lives of the masses.

The Bible says that such men are full of deceitful words (Psalm 36:3). Their counsel is deceitful (Proverbs 12:5). Their favor is deceitful (Proverbs 27:6). And their hearts are deceitful (Mark 7:22). They defraud the unsuspecting (Romans 16:18), displaying the spirit of anti-Christ (2 John 7), all for the sake of wealth, prestige, and prerogative (Proverbs 21:6).

Such puissance is in the long run all too fleeting, however (Revelation 21:8), because mythmakers do not go unpunished (Proverbs 19:5). Ultimately, their sin finds them out (Jeremiah 17:11).

Still, because their lies wreak havoc among the innocent (Micah 6:12), it is essential that we not be taken in. Not only are we to be alert to deception (Ephesians 4:14), testing the words and deeds of the mythmakers against the Truth (1 John 4:1-6), but we are to expose their deceptions as well (Ephesians 5:11).

Margaret Sanger—and her heirs at Planned Parenthood—not at all unlike Jeroboam and the other infamous mythmakers throughout history, have thus far been able to parlay deception into a substantial empire. But now, the truth must be told. The illusion must be exposed. The Big Lie must be demythologized.

Therefore, go and tell.

"Woe to the bloody city, completely full of lies and pillage. Her prey never departs." (Nahum 3:1).

Endnotes

ACKNOWLEDGMENTS
1. *Illustrated London News*, August 19, 1921.
2. Hilaire Belloc, *The Path to Rome*. London: Cassell's, 1908, p. 4.

INTRODUCTION
1. *Illustrated London News*, December 23, 1933.
2. Harold Tribble Cole, *The Coming Terror*. New York: Languine, 1936, p. 23.
3. *Coronet Magazine*, March 1966.
4. Abraham Storn, *The Margaret Sanger Story*. Westport, Conn.: Greenwood Press, 1975.
5. Madeline Gray, *Margaret Sanger: A Biography of the Champion of Birth Control*. New York: Richard Marek, 1979.
6. Zachary Keen, *The Art of History*. New York: Ball and Brothers, 1948, p. 34.
7. Hilaire Belloc, *The Biographer's Art: Excerpts from Belloc's Florrid Pen*. London: Catholic Union, 1956, p. 33.
8. Howard F. Pallin, ed., *Literary English and Scottish Sermons*. London: Windus Etheridge, 1937, p. 101.
9. E. Michael Jones, *Degenerate Moderns: Modernity as Rationalized Sexual Misbehavior*. San Francisco: Ignatius Press, 1993, p. 9.
10. Planned Parenthood Federation of America, "1992 Annual Report," p. 21.

11. Gray, *Margaret Sanger*.
12. PPFA, "Annual Report," p. 21.
13. Ibid., p. 19.
14. Ibid.; Also see, International Planned Parenthood Federation, "1991 Annual Report," p. 22; Also see, National STOPP News, November 30, 1993.
15. Douglas R. Scott, *Bad Choices: A Look Inside Planned Parenthood*. Franklin, Tenn.: Legacy Communications, 1992, p. 29.
16. George Grant, *Grand Illusions: The Legacy of Planned Parenthood*. Franklin, Tenn.: Legacy, 1988, 1992; also, Nashville, Tenn.: Cumberland House, 2000.

CHAPTER 1

1. *Illustrated London News*, October 29, 1910.
2. *Illustrated London News*, September 26, 1908.
3. James Killarney, *Fulcrum of Vision*. New York: Jamison, Talmidge, and Yeates, 1956, p. 458.
4. Gray, p. 19.
5. Ibid., p. 21.
6. Ibid., p. 16.
7. Ibid., p. 18.
8. Ibid.
9. Margaret Sanger, *An Autobiography*. New York: Dover, 1938.

CHAPTER 2

1. *Illustrated London News*, March 15, 1919.
2. Gray, *Margaret Sanger*, p. 38.
3. Ibid., p. 43.
4. Ibid.
5. Herman Schwartz, *Margaret Sanger: A Biography*. New York: Bell Tower, 1968, p. 44.
6. Ibid., p. 48.

CHAPTER 3

1. *Illustrated London News*, March 9, 1918.
2. *Illustrated London News*, August 16, 1930.
3. Lester McHenry, *Fanatical Ideas: A History of the American Left*. New York: Dillard Willings, 1931.
4. Francis X. Gannon, *A Biographical Dictionary of the Left*.

Belmont, Mass.: Western Islands, 1973, IV: p. 313.
5. Ibid., p. 317.
6. Ibid.
7. McHenry, *Fanatical Ideas*, p. 88.
8. Gannon, *Biographical Dictionary* IV: p. 313.
9. Ibid., p. 182.

CHAPTER 4

1. *Illustrated London News*, May 14, 1932.
2. Gray, pp. 58–59.

CHAPTER 5

1. *Illustrated London News*, October 2, 1920.
2. *Illustrated London News*, April 14, 1917.
3. McHenry, *Fanatical Ideas,* p. 129.
4. James Cotton, *Paris.* London: Fallows Press, 1988, p. 36.
5. Albert Gringer, *The Sanger Corpus: A Study in Militancy.* Lakeland, Ala.: Lakeland Christian College, 1974, p. 473.
6. Ibid.
7. Ibid., p. 477.
8. Ibid., p. 481.
9. Ibid., p. 488.
10. William H. Bradenton, *The Comstock Era: The Reformation of Reform.* New York: Laddel Press, 1958, p. 276.
11. Gringer, *The Sanger Corpus*, p. 489.

CHAPTER 6

1. *Illustrated London News*, May 14, 1927.
2. Allan Chase, *The Legacy of Malthus: The Social Costs of the New Scientific Racism.* New York: Knopf, 1977, p. 7.
3. Paul Johnson, *A History of the English People.* New York: Harper and Row, 1985, p. 276.
4. Ibid.
5. Germaine Greer, *Sex and Destiny.* New York: Harper and Row, 1984, p. 309.
6. Daniel Kevels, *In the Name of Eugenics.* New York: Penguin, 1985, p. 110.
7. Ibid.
8. *Illustrated London News*, February 14, 1925.
9. Ibid.

10. G. K. Chesterton, *Eugenics and Other Evils*. London: Cassell, 1922, p. 54.

CHAPTER 7

1. *Illustrated London News*, September 27, 1919.
2. *Illustrated London News*, January 9, 1909.
3. Linda Gordon, *Woman's Body, Woman's Right*. New York: Penguin, 1974, p. 204.
4. Ibid.
5. Margaret Sanger, *The Pivot of Civilization*. New York: Brentano's, 1922, p. 101.
6. Ibid., p. 108.
7. Ibid., p. 123.

CHAPTER 8

1. *Illustrated London News*, December 4, 1920.
2. *Washington Times*, February 3, 1988.
3. Sanger, *The Pivot of Civilization*, pp. 23, 107, 126.
4. David Kennedy, *Birth Control in America: The Career of Margaret Sanger*. New Haven, Conn.: Yale, 1970, pp. 113–118.
5. Gordon, *Woman's Body, Woman's Right*, pp. 229–234.
6. Ibid., p. 332.
7. Ibid.
8. Ibid.
9. Ibid.
10. Ibid., p. 333.

CHAPTER 9

1. *Illustrated London News*, November 12, 1932.
2. *Illustrated London News*, October 21, 1905.
3. Margaret Sanger, ed., *International Aspects of Birth Control: The International Neo-Malthusian and Birth Control Conference*. New York: American Birth Control League, 1925, p. v.
4. Ibid., p. 5.
5. Ibid.
6. Ibid., p. 146.
7. *Science 82*, March 1982.
8. Family Planning Perspectives, June 1970.

9. IPPF, *Annual Report*, 1983.
10. IPPF, *Family Planning Handbook for Doctors*, 1987.
11. IPPF, *A Strategy for Legal Change*, 1981.

CHAPTER 10

1. *Illustrated London News*, October 8, 1910.
2. Scott, *Bad Choices*, pp. 233–270.
3. Ibid., pp. 159–166.

CHAPTER 11

1. *Illustrated London News*, April 19, 1924.
2. *Illustrated London News*, August 5, 1933.
3. *The Humanist*, July 1986.
4. Margaret Sanger, *Woman and the New Race*. New York: George Halter, 1928, p. 67.
5. Gray, *Margaret Sanger*, p. 88.
6. *Wall Street Journal*, December 19, 1984.
7. Leon Trotsky, *My Life*. New York: Scribner's, 1931, p. 274.
8. David Goldstein, *Suicide Bent*. Saint Paul, Minn.: Radio Replies, 1945, p. 72.
9. Planned Parenthood of Houston, *Annual Report*, 1985.

CHAPTER 12

1. *Illustrated London News*, May 16, 1936.
2. *USA Today*, March 8, 1995.
3. Michael Scott Horton, *Mission Accomplished*. Nashville: Nelson, 1986, p. 11.

Printed in the USA
CPSIA information can be obtained
at www.ICGtesting.com
JSHW082359140824
68134JS00020B/2175